TAPPING INTO
# Wisdom's Treasures

DAVID SHEARIN

Unless otherwise indicated, Scripture quotations are taken from the New King James Version of the Bible. Used by permission of Thomas Nelson Publishing. All rights reserved.

The Amplified Bible. Used by permission of Zondervan Publishing. All rights reserved.

Arthur S. Way. The Letters of St. Paul to Seven Churches and Three Friends with the Letter to the Hebrews., Published by Kregel Publications, Grand Rapids, MI. Used by permission of the publisher. All rights reserved.

The James Moffatt Translation. Public Domain

S.C. Carpenter D.D., The letter to the Ephesians, A Paraphrase. Public Domain

John Taylor, A Paraphrase with Notes on the Epistle to the Romans. Public Domain

Helen Barrett Montgomery, Centenary Translation of the New Testament. Public Domain

New Living Translation, copyright © 1996, 2004, 2007, 2013 by Tyndale House Foundation. Used by permission of Tyndale House Publishers, Inc., Carol Stream, Illinois 60188. All rights reserved.

William Barclay, The New Testament Volume II, Published by Westminster John Knox Press. Used by permission of the publisher. All rights reserved.

# Acknowledgements

I would like to acknowledge with deepest gratitude…

My wife Vicki and daughter Ashley who have sacrificed greatly for me to be able to fulfill the call of God upon my life.

My mother Lannie Shearin, now in heaven whose prayers and godly example have given me stability in every season of my life.

My spiritual fathers, Reverend Kenneth E. ("Dad") Hagin and Pastor B.B. Hankins, who are cheering me on from the grandstands of heaven.

My pastors for nearly forty years, Phil and Barbara Privette.

Mark and Trina Hankins, who have been true friends and spiritual mentors to Vicki and me for more than thirty years.

My staff, whose assistance and support was so vital in the writing of *Tapping Into Wisdom's Treasures*.

# Contents

Introduction . . . . . . . . . . . . . . . . . . . . . . . . 6

Chapter 1: The One Thing that
             Makes All the Difference . . . . . . . . . . . . . 7

Chapter 2: Are You Drilling . . . . . . . . . . . . . . . . . . . . . . 27

Chapter 3: Like a Tree by the Water . . . . . . . . . . . . . . 45

Chapter 4: Winning the Tug-O-War . . . . . . . . . . . . . . . 63

Chapter 5: Get Quiet and Listen . . . . . . . . . . . . . . . . . 81

Chapter 6: The Secret of Supernatural Success . . . . . 99

Scriptures . . . . . . . . . . . . . . . . . . . . . . . . . . . . . . . . 117

About the Author . . . . . . . . . . . . . . . . . . . . . . . . . 128

# Introduction

Do you ever find yourself in situations where you feel like you don't have the wisdom to handle them? Have you ever made a wrong business decision? Wrong investment? Have you ever gotten involved with the wrong person? Or made an agreement with somebody that didn't carry out his or her end of the agreement? Like you, I have felt lost and have not always known what to do in every situation or how to respond to every circumstance that has come my way. But I always confess that I know what to do. Why? God made Jesus wisdom to us. Just like the bay and the ocean are one. The same water in the ocean is the water that flows into the bay. The same life that is in Christ flows into you today as a believer in union with Jesus Christ. The same wisdom that is in Christ flows into your spirit and you can tap into it. You can draw from the wisdom of God that is stored up in the person of Jesus Christ. The Scripture says, "Counsel in the heart of man is like deep water, but a man of understanding will draw it out." There is counsel in your heart. There is a wealth of wisdom, but you must learn to tap into and to receive that wisdom.

In this book *Tapping Into Wisdom's Treasure* I will give you five practical ways to tap into the wealth of divine wisdom and knowledge that belongs to you in Christ. The Holy Spirit will give you access into God's wisdom so you will be able to see the way that God sees your situation. God's wisdom will show you what to do, when to do it, how to do it, and with whom to do it, so you can make the right decisions, get the right results, and God's blessing will be on your life!

# Chapter 1

## The *One Thing* that Makes All the Difference

*On that night God appeared to Solomon, and said to him, "Ask! What shall I give you?"*
                              2 Chronicles 1:7

What would you say if God asked you the question He asked Solomon?

Seriously. Consider it for a moment.

Imagine the Creator of the universe appeared to you tonight, woke you out of a sound sleep, and offered to give you whatever you want. As you shook the cobwebs from your head and rubbed your astonished eyes, how would you respond? What would you request?

Before you answer, let me give you a hint. There's

## TAPPING INTO WISDOM'S TREASURES

one particular request you could make that would outshine any other. It's a request that, once granted, would abundantly enrich every area of your life. It would reveal solutions to your most perplexing problems. It would enable you to turn troubles into triumphs. And it would put within your reach every good thing you could ever desire—not just temporarily, but for the rest of your life.

What request could possibly cover so much ground? The one Solomon made in 2 Chronicles 1:10:

"O Lord God...give me wisdom and knowledge!"

That is definitely a very powerful prayer. When Solomon prayed it, God responded in a big way. He not only made Solomon the wisest man in the world, He turned him into the richest and one of the most honored kings in the Old Testament.

In light of that fact, you'd expect everybody who ever read the Bible to follow his example. You'd think believers everywhere would constantly be praying what Solomon prayed. But that's not necessarily what's happening. As Christians pray about the challenges of everyday life, Solomon's request isn't always the first thing that comes to their minds.

Instead, they're likely to ask for other things. They might think about the financial challenges they're facing and ask God for money or a better paying job. They might think about the unfulfilled dreams in their heart and ask Him for opportunity, or influence, or honor.

I don't mean to imply that Christians don't ever ask God for wisdom at all. Eventually, most of us get around to it. It just might not be the first request on our list.

Why is that? Because wisdom is greatly undervalued these days. Although we as believers know it's a good thing, we don't always think of it as the best or most important thing in life. Yet God says that's exactly what it is. He tells us clearly in the Bible:

> Wisdom is the principal thing; therefore get wisdom. And in all your getting, get understanding. Exalt her, and she will promote you; she will bring you honor, when you embrace her. She will place on your head an ornament of grace; a crown of glory she will deliver to you." (Prov. 4:7-9)
>
> Happy is the man who finds wisdom, and the man who gains understanding; for her proceeds are better than the profits of silver, and her gain than fine gold. She is more precious than rubies, and all the things you may desire cannot compare with her. Length of days is in her right hand, in her left hand riches and honor. Her ways are ways of pleasantness, and all her paths are peace. She is a tree of life to those who take hold of her, and happy are all who retain her. (Prov. 3:13-18)

Talk about a wonderful life! What more could anyone want than grace, glory, promotion, honor, long life, riches, happiness, pleasantness, and peace? That's the kind of life we all dream of! And the Bible says it can be ours if

we will do this one thing:
*Get wisdom.*

When we have enough of God's wisdom and we live according to it we can, as the saying goes, *Have it all!* We can experience the fullest measure of what Jesus has provided for us through the plan of redemption. We can truly live the abundant life.[1]

## Direct from the Storehouse to You

"But Pastor David," you might say, "I'm not like Solomon. I'm just a normal person. Could such extraordinary wisdom really be available to me?"

Certainly!

God's will from the beginning has been to make it available to all mankind. You can see that by looking at how God created Adam. He made him in His own image, put His own life in him, and endowed him with enough divine understanding and intelligence to exercise dominion over the whole earth. One of Adam's first jobs was to name every creature in the animal kingdom. Think about the creativity and insight that required! It was a monumental task. Yet Adam was up to it because he had an absolutely amazing intellect.

Adam's brilliance would have remained fully intact and the entire human race would have inherited it if he'd stuck with God's original plan. But, sadly, he didn't. Instead,

---

[1] John 10:10: "The thief does not come except to steal, and to kill, and to destroy. I have come that they may have life, and that they may have it more abundantly."

he chose to sin. Through sin, spiritual death and mortality came, and much of humanity's intellectual brilliance and creativity was destroyed.

That was a tragedy, no question about it. But, as you well know, it's not the end of the story. Sin didn't get to have the last word. Jesus did.

He came to earth and purchased our redemption. In His death, He was made to be our sin. He became what we were, died in our place as our substitute, and paid the sin-debt we owed but could not pay. Then, through His resurrection, He restored everything we lost. He became the first of a whole different breed, the firstborn of an entirely new race of humanity.

As "the last Adam,"[2] Jesus became the Storehouse, so to speak, of everything God wanted mankind to be. All God's divine attributes were invested in Him, then we were given the opportunity to be born again in Him so that *in Christ* we can be everything He is and have everything He has. As the New Testament says:

- For in Him dwells all the fullness of the Godhead bodily; and you are complete in Him. (Col. 2:9)

- For He [God] made Him who knew no sin to be sin for us, that we might become the righteousness of God in Him. (2 Cor. 5:21)

- Therefore, if anyone is in Christ, he is a new creation; old things have passed away;

---
2  1 Corinthians 15:45

behold, all things have become new. Now all things are of God. (2 Cor. 5:17-18)

In my book, The Master Key, we explored what it means to be a "new creation" in Christ. We learned that in Him we have an entirely new identity. We're no longer descendants of fallen Adam with a sin-darkened nature. We've been spiritually reborn into the family of God. More than just forgiven sinners who've turned over a new leaf; we've become another kind of leaf altogether on a completely different kind of tree.

As born again believers, we're just as much God's sons and daughters as Jesus is because we've been joined spiritually to Him. We've become one with Him. Just as a vine and a branch are united, and the life that's in one flows into the other, so through our union with Jesus, His divine life flows into us.[3] As a result, we share His character and His identity. We have, flowing into us, everything He possesses.

Including His wisdom!

As stunning as it might seem, 1 Corinthians 1:29-31 confirms this. There, the Bible says:

> ...No flesh should glory in His presence. But of Him you are in Christ Jesus, who became for us wisdom from God; and righteousness and sanctification and redemption; that, as it is written, He who glories, let him glory in the LORD.

---
3 John 15:5: "I am the vine, you are the branches. He who abides in Me, and I in him, bears much fruit; for without Me you can do nothing."

Just think of it! The very wisdom of God Himself—wisdom more fathomless than the deepest ocean—is stored up in Christ; and because you are in Him, that wisdom belongs to you. It flows into your spirit like the waters of the ocean flow into the bay.

## Which Option Will You Choose?

I know what you're probably thinking right now. *If the wisdom of God has been flowing into me ever since I became Christian, why do I so often feel like I don't know what I'm doing? Why do I still have so many unanswered questions about certain areas of my life?*

Because God's wisdom doesn't just fall on you automatically like rain falls from the sky. It resides on the inside of you like a wellspring of water in your spirit. Therefore, you have to learn how to tap into it to enjoy its benefits.

Proverbs 20:5 puts it this way. It says: "Counsel in the heart of man is like deep water, but a man of understanding will draw it out." Although that's an Old Testament verse, it's doubly true for you as a New Testament believer. You not only have God's counsel in your heart, you have the ultimate Counselor, the Holy Spirit, living inside you. Jesus sent Him to live in your spirit and teach you all things.[4]

The Holy Spirit is your divine helper and guide. He's ready and willing at all times to cause the deep waters

---

4 John 14:26: But the Comforter, which is the Holy Ghost, whom the Father will send in my name, he shall teach you all things, and bring all things to your remembrance, whatsoever I have said unto you.

of God's wisdom to surface in your heart so you can make right choices and decisions at every point in your life. But to effectively draw out His counsel, there are certain basic truths you must understand.

You must realize, for instance, there are two types of wisdom described in the Scripture. The first is God's wisdom. It "comes from above," and is described in the New Testament as "first pure, then peaceable, gentle, willing to yield, full of mercy and good fruits, without partiality and without hypocrisy."[5] The second kind of wisdom "does not descend from above, but is earthly, sensual, demonic."[6] It originates with the devil and is communicated to us through the flesh and the influences of this ungodly world.

As Christians we have two options. We can either listen to God and draw our wisdom from Him by the Spirit; or we can listen to our flesh and draw our wisdom from the world. God has given us the freedom to do either one. But the Bible leaves no doubt about which option He wants us to choose. It says: "Not from men but from God...draw your life in Messiah Jesus who became for us God-given wisdom."[7] In other words, don't get your wisdom from the earthly, devilish realm. Don't get it from your flesh or put your confidence in the counsel of this corrupt world. Get your wisdom from Christ!

Exactly how do we go about getting wisdom from Christ?

We start with the Bible. As the written Word of God,

---
5  James 3:17
6  James 3:15
7  1 Corinthians 1:30, Arthur S. Way

*The One Thing that Makes All the Difference*

it contains His wisdom. We extract that wisdom by reading the Word, meditating on it, and letting the Holy Spirit reveal its meaning to our heart. The process is very simple, really. But there is one hitch.

The devil constantly fights us over it. He knows how much divine power and blessing God's wisdom makes available to us, so he's always trying to steal it from us by separating us from God's Word. That's been his strategy ever since the Garden of Eden. The first time he used it was with Eve. Do you remember the story?. The devil approached Eve through the serpent, started questioning God's Word, and convinced her to doubt it.

"Has God indeed said, 'You shall not eat of every tree of the garden'?" he asked.

> And the woman said to the serpent, "We may eat the fruit of the trees of the garden; but of the fruit of the tree which is in the midst of the garden, God has said, 'You shall not eat it, nor shall you touch it, lest you die.'" Then the serpent said to the woman, "You will not surely die. For God knows that in the day you eat of it your eyes will be opened, and you will be like God, knowing good and evil." So when the woman saw that the tree was good for food, that it was pleasant to the eyes, and a tree desirable to make one wise, she took of its fruit and ate. She also gave to her husband with her, and he ate. (Genesis 3:1-6)

I'm sure the Holy Spirit was trying to intervene in

that conversation the whole time and help Eve make the right choice. But she didn't listen to Him. She silenced His voice inside her by disregarding the Word of God. As a result, both she and Adam made a decision that was based not on the wisdom from above but on fleshly, demonic wisdom.

The consequences were catastrophic. Adam and Eve fell from their place of divine dominion in the realm of the spirit to a place of bondage to the devil in the realm of the flesh. They exchanged life and blessing for death and the curse. They lost their inner access to the wisdom of God and nothing was ever the same for them again.

## A Stratospherically Spectacular View

If the devil had gotten his way, you and I would still be living in that fallen state today. We'd be bound to this natural realm and have no ability at all to see beyond what's happening in the flesh. Just like sinful Adam and Eve, we'd be cut off from God, and incapable of seeing anything from His point of view.

But that's not the case! For those of us who are in Christ Jesus, the curse of sin has been reversed. We've been lifted up above the lowlands of the devil. God has "made us alive together with Christ (by grace you have been saved), and raised us up together, and made us sit together in the heavenly places in Christ Jesus."[8] Just like in the beginning in the Garden of Eden, we have access to His wisdom again.

The word translated *wisdom* in the New Testament

---
8 Ephesians 2:5-6

is the Greek word, *sophia*, which means *insight into the true nature of things*. It refers to the ability to see things from an insightful perspective.

Does seeing things from God's perspective make a difference? Absolutely!

Think about it this way. If I walk out the front door of our church, stand on the sidewalk and look around, my field of vision is very limited. I can see what's straight in front of me directly across the street. I can turn my head to the left and to the right and see what's on either side of me. But that's about all. If I went downtown to the Stratosphere, however, which is the tallest free standing tower in the United States, rode the elevator to the top and stood in the observation area, I'd get an entirely different perspective. I'd get the big picture. I'd be able to see for miles in every direction and have a lot more insight into how this city is laid out.

When it comes to our perspective on life, much the same thing is true. If we look at things simply from a fleshly point of view it's like standing at street level. All we can see is what's happening around us in this natural, physical realm. All we know is what somebody else tells us, or how our emotions are reacting, or what we experienced in the past when we were in this situation. When we base our decisions on that kind of limited insight we often make the wrong ones.

But when we come up where God is calling us to be, we get a stratospherically spectacular view. In the Spirit, through our union with Christ, our perception is heightened.

## TAPPING INTO WISDOM'S TREASURES

We're able to look beyond our natural circumstances, the pressures we're feeling, and what's happened to us in the past. We can see our situation from God's perspective and consequently make the right decisions.

God's wisdom makes all the difference! When you tap into it, you know things that are unknowable without it. Mysteries are revealed to you that have been hidden from your understanding.

Although you still have full use of your natural intelligence and the reasoning abilities God has given you, a higher intelligence is added to them. The Holy Spirit places His *super* on your *natural*. As a result, you can see things you couldn't otherwise see and do things you couldn't otherwise do. You're able to accomplish dreams and goals that, without God's wisdom, you could never accomplish.

### An Avalanche of Wisdom and Prudence

As exciting as all this sounds, you may not feel right now like such supernatural wisdom is really available to you. Maybe you can't remember ever having tapped into it at all. But if you're born again, it's yours nonetheless—and it's yours in abundance!

The Bible leaves no doubt about this. It says to all of us who are in Christ:

- In Him we have redemption through His blood, the forgiveness of sins, according to the riches of His grace which He made to abound toward us in all wisdom and prudence. (Eph. 1:7-8)

- God's grace...has overflowed upon us in a full stream of wisdom and discernment. (Knox Translation)

- The heavens were opened and all the gifts of God descended, abounding and cascading on us, wisdom to know that which had been unknowable. (Carpenter Translation)

Notice, those scriptures don't tell us that God has given us just a little cup full of His wisdom. They don't say He's sprinkled us with just barely enough to get by. They assure us He's poured it out on us like a flood.

If you want to see where that flood comes from, read Revelation 22:1. It tells about "a pure river of water of life, clear as crystal, proceeding from the throne of God and of the Lamb." God's wisdom is part of the river. It's always flowing to us in abundance, flooding our spirit with His life, and making known to us, in a full and never-ending stream, the hidden knowledge of His will.

Picture that river in your mind right now and see it rushing right from God's throne into your spirit. Think of it, as one of the above translations put it, "cascading" down into your heart. The word *cascading* speaks of what happens in the mountains when there's so much snow it comes tumbling down in an avalanche. I've never witnessed this in person, but on television I've seen people skiing down a hill with an avalanche chasing behind them. The avalanche, which moves faster than the skiers can, always overtakes them. It engulfs them and covers them up. That's how Ephesians 1:8 describes the "wisdom and prudence" that's ours in Christ!

As we've already established, the Greek word for wisdom refers to God's insight and perspective. It's what enables us to see what He sees. The word *prudence* takes us a step further. Translated from the Greek word *phronecius* it refers to the ability to discern modes of action with a view to their results.

That's a valuable ability! Prudence can keep you from making decisions in life you'll later regret. It can enable you to foresee the unexpected negative consequences of those decisions so you can change your course of action. Then you can make better choices and save yourself a lot of trouble.

When you have wisdom and prudence together you not only know what to do, you know when to do it, how to do it, and with whom it should be done. You're able to make a plan, carry it out, and foresee what's going to happen as a result. You know in advance that it's the right plan and it will be productive. It will be a blessing and not a mistake.

Have you ever made a business decision, thinking at the time it was right, and it turned out to be wrong? Have you ever done the right thing but with the wrong motive, or at the wrong time? Timing is everything. Ask the rabbit that crossed the road. Have you ever gotten involved with people you thought were trustworthy and it turned out they weren't?

Yes, you have. I have too. At times, we've all neglected to tap into the wisdom of God. We've all paid the painful price and suffered the consequences that come from operating according to the lower, worldly kind of wisdom rather than the wisdom that comes from above. But we don't have to keep paying that price. We don't have to keep suffering those consequences.

In Christ, we can choose another way. We can get God's perspective. We can avail ourselves of His wisdom and prudence and make the right decision at the right time with the right motive and the right people.

We can know what to do even when, from a strictly natural perspective, *we don't know what to do!*

## When Pressure Can't Push You Around

Personally, I have a lot of experience with this. Both as a pastor and as a Christian, I often find myself in situations I feel I don't have the natural wisdom to handle. But when I encounter those situations, because the Bible teaches we have what we say, I don't talk about how I feel. Instead, I declare the truth of God's Word. I say, "I know what to do. I know when to do it. And I know how to do it." Then I trust God to give me the necessary knowledge, wisdom, and prudence to make the best decision and do what needs to be done.

I'm remembering right now one particular time, decades ago, when my wife and I were just getting started in ministry. We were fresh out of Bible college and, although we didn't have much of anything else, we had a word from the Lord. "Go to Las Vegas and start a church." So we packed our few, well-worn belongings into a little U-Haul truck and moved to Las Vegas.

When we arrived there we had no place to live, no promise of an income, and a fledgling congregation of only five people. I looked in the newspaper for houses to rent, but because of our circumstances, I had no budget to guide me. (You can't figure out a budget when you don't have any money.) So I zeroed in on the cheapest rental house I could find.

I called about it and made an appointment to see it. The man I spoke to on the phone made it clear he expected me to show up for the appointment. In a voice as rough as sandpaper he said, "Don't leave me high and dry!"

I didn't. I showed up right on time. But I left quickly. The house was not one I wanted to live in. (I still shudder when I remember the color of the carpet.) "I think I can believe God for something higher than this!" I said to myself. But no other houses were available for that price. Although we could have found an apartment, I didn't want to live in an apartment. I wanted a house. I wanted to be able to stomp around, praise God, and pray out loud without somebody in the next apartment banging on the wall and saying, "Hey, quiet down over there!" That's what I desired, and God said I could have what I desire.[9] So our house hunt continued.

The house we eventually settled on was a new one located in a new neighborhood. The owner was asking $525

---

9  Psalm 37:4: Delight yourself also in the LORD, And He shall give you the desires of your heart.

a month in rent. My wife and I had asked the Lord to give us wisdom about how much rent we should pay and He put the figure of $450 in both of our hearts. This is how much we had faith for, so we had to negotiate with the owner.

Negotiating over $70 may not sound like a major deal, but for me it was big because I didn't have any money at all. What I did have, though, was faith. I believed I'd heard from God and I had His wisdom and favor. So I called the owner, a wealthy man who owned a lot of homes and commercial properties, and said, "We want to rent this house, and we can pay you $450." He said he was willing to come down to $495. I asked if we could meet him in person to discuss it. He agreed and we arranged a meeting.

He stuck firm to his price. "The rent is $495," he said.

I stuck firm too. "We want to rent it for $450," I repeated.

"Okay, I'll rent it to you for three months at that price and then the rent will go up."

"No. I want it for $450."

We went back and forth for a while until he finally stood up, stuck his hand out to shake mine and said, "All right! You can have it for $450."

We lived in that house for five years and the rent never changed. Even though the owners went through some difficult times, they never increased it.

See how practical God's wisdom is? It will help you in every area of life. Whether you're just getting started like we were back then, or you've gone on to greater things

## TAPPING INTO WISDOM'S TREASURES

and higher levels, if you'll tap into God's wisdom, He will direct you. He'll give you His insight and prudence so that your judgment won't be skewed by the pressures of the world.

Pressure often pushes people into making poor choices and decisions. But God's wisdom will keep pressure from pushing you around. It will keep you steady, direct you, and get you where you need to be, right on time. It will show you what to do, when to do it, how to do it, and with whom to do it, so you can make the right decisions, get the right results, and God's blessing will be on your life.

No wonder the Bible says: *Get wisdom!*

## *Confession*

Because I'm in Christ, God's grace abounds toward me in all wisdom and prudence. I have God's insight into things and can see from His perspective. I know what to do. I know when to do it. I know how to do it, and I know with whom to do it. I can make the right decisions and get the right results!

## *Summary Questions*

1. Why does the Bible say that wisdom is the principle thing?

2. How do we know that it's God's will for us to have His wisdom?

3. How would you describe the two different kinds of wisdom?

4. Where is the first place we should look for God's wisdom?

5. Based on the Greek definitions of the words translated *wisdom* and *prudence* in the New Testament, how can they be of benefit to you in your daily life?

# Chapter 2
## Are You Drilling?

*For the LORD gives wisdom; From His mouth come knowledge and understanding; He stores up sound wisdom for the upright.*

Proverbs 2:6-7

In Christ, you are wealthy beyond your wildest dreams. You may not fully realize it yet (most Christians don't), but it's the absolute truth.

Through the plan of redemption, God has opened up a spiritual bank account for you. He has deposited into it everything Jesus is, everything He possesses, and everything He did through His death and resurrection. He's made you Jesus' joint heir and given you full access to His resources. And as we established in the previous chapter, one of those resources is wisdom.

## TAPPING INTO WISDOM'S TREASURES

I don't know about you, but if somebody opened an account in my name at the local bank, I'd be excited about it. I'd be eager to take advantage of what I'd been given. I'd also have two very important questions:

1. How much money is in the account?

2. How do I get access to it?

As believers, we need to ask those same questions about our spiritual account. We need to find out exactly what's in it and how we go about drawing it out. We can do this by looking in the Bible. It's filled with revelation about our divine inheritance, and here's what it says about how much wisdom belongs to us in Christ:

"In him lie hidden *all* the treasures of wisdom and knowledge." (Col. 2:3, NLT)

The word *all* is a big word. It means there's nothing left out; everything is included. In this context it indicates that not just part of God's wisdom and knowledge but the full measure of it is in Christ. He has complete access to God's perspective and insight into the true nature of things. Everything God thinks, the way He sees things, and everything anybody could ever need to know about anything is all in Jesus.

This means the resources in our divine account are literally infinite. There's no limit to how much of God's wisdom we can have—which is a good thing because we need a lot of it in order to live a truly abundant life. On our own, we don't know how. All we have is the information

## Are You Drilling?

we've gleaned from this natural world and what we've experienced in the past. Natural information, at best, is woefully inadequate. At worst, it negatively skews our perspective. Either way, it doesn't provide us with what it takes to live a really victorious, God kind of life.

Sadly, many Christians don't realize this. They think that just because they're highly educated they have all the wisdom they need. But they're badly mistaken.

Education by itself, as valuable as it is, doesn't make a person wise. True wisdom comes only by the Word and the Spirit of God. There was a time in America when people knew this and the Bible was central to our nation's educational system. It was actually a part of the curriculum. Students were encouraged to study it and make their ultimate quest to know God and the Lord Jesus Christ. A number of American universities were established for this very purpose.

But today our educational system has veered far off track. Elementary schools, high schools, and colleges all over this country have banned Biblical references from their classrooms. They've turned away from God. As a result, the development of our culture in recent years has been based upon ignorance of God rather than knowledge of Him.

Since "the wisdom of this world is foolishness with God,"[10] (or, as one translation puts it, "nonsense in God's sight")[11] that's what this world's culture has produced: a lot

---

10  1 Corinthians 3:19
11  Ibid, God's Word Translation

of foolish nonsense that has taken people down a wrong path. But as believers we don't have to walk that path. God has lifted us above it. He's seated us with Christ in heavenly places. We no longer have to allow the world to shape us into its mold and tell us what to think and how to see things. We don't have to let it distort our perceptions and imprison us by its perspective.

We've been set free. God has opened the eyes of our understanding and given us unlimited access to His own, divine wisdom: a wisdom that's too great to be contained in any classroom. An infinite wisdom that knows no bounds.

## Hidden for You Not from You

"But Pastor David," you might say, "the verse from Colossians you quoted says that in Christ 'lie *hidden* all the treasures of wisdom and knowledge.' If God really wants me to have this wisdom, why has He hidden it from me?"

He hasn't hidden it *from* you. He's hidden it *for* you! By storing it up in Christ, He's put it in a place where you can find it and the devil can't. Time and again the New Testament explains this. It tells us that God conceals His wisdom from Satan and his followers but reveals it to those of us who are in Christ.

That's what happened when Jesus went to the cross. The devil had no understanding at all about what was going on. He thought, by crucifying Jesus, he'd be able to get rid of Him. He thought he was doing something great for himself by killing God's Son. But he turned out to be dead wrong. What he was actually doing was carrying out God's plan. He was setting it up so that men could be saved and Jesus could multiply Himself through them a million times over by making it possible for them to be born again.

1 Corinthians 2:7-8 says this was "the hidden wisdom which God ordained before the ages for our glory, which none of the rulers of this age knew; for had they known, they would not have crucified the Lord of glory."

Think about the dynamic power of God's divine wisdom! It takes the devil's attempts at destruction, turns them around, and brings restoration out of them. That's what happened on the cross some 2,000 years ago, and it can happen in your life today. Through His wisdom, God can take what the devil used to harm you and make it work for your good. He can redeem the shattered areas of your life and make them better than they were before they were broken, because He knows how to put things back together. He knows how to recreate things in your life and make them new.

With the wisdom God has stored and hidden in Christ for us, God can completely undermine the devil's best laid plans. He can get every one of us, as believers, in the right place at the right time with the right people doing the right thing. No matter what obstacles the devil throws in front of us, with God's wisdom we can overcome!

Why, then, aren't more Christians overcoming? Because there's a problem. You can see what it is in Colossians 2:3. It says that "in [Christ] lie hidden all the

## TAPPING INTO WISDOM'S TREASURES

mighty *untapped* treasures of wisdom and knowledge."[12] The word *untapped* there is the key. It indicates that even though all the riches of divine wisdom belong to us in Christ, we can experience a shortage if we let that wisdom remain hidden.

Think of it in terms of a natural resource, like oil for instance. People sometimes say there's a shortage of oil when there's actually not. Oil is available in vast quantities. There's more of it than we can imagine hidden underground all over the earth. The resource is there. The problem is there aren't enough people drilling wells and pumping it out.

In other words, there's no shortage of oil. There's a shortage of drilling.

The same is true about the mighty untapped treasures of God's wisdom and knowledge. The resource is there. More than we could ever need is available to us in abundance. The question is: Are Christians drilling? Are they tapping into that resource and drawing it up out of their heart?

No, to be quite blunt about it, many believers aren't. They're just sitting around watching secular television. Nobody ever got the wisdom of God from watching a bunch of ungodly TV shows. All those shows have to offer is the wisdom of the world.

I'm not saying you should never watch TV. Just don't put your mind in a non-thinking mode and allow the world's system to flood you with its philosophy and ideas.

---
12  Colossians 2:3, Taylor's Living Bible

Don't drop your guard and let the world do your thinking for you. If you do that, your perspective will be infected by the kind of earthly, sensual, demonic wisdom that's the very opposite of the wisdom of God.

This is one reason why our nation is in such sad shape these days. The Hollywood mindset has altered our whole culture. Music has too. Ungodly thoughts are turned into songs and people sing them; they absorb those thoughts and the philosophy behind them. Their perspective is altered and, ultimately, so is our nation.

It's happening all the time, all around us. But as believers, we're not supposed to be a part of it. We're not called to just soak up the world's wisdom and mindlessly absorb its influences. God wants us to combat those influences by thinking like He does and seeing like He sees. He wants the church to drill down into the treasures of His wisdom and knowledge and gain understanding from His Word so that we can live in total contrast to the world's mindset. Then we can alter our culture for the good. We can influence it for Jesus.

"Is such a thing really possible?" you might ask. "Can we as believers really make a godly difference in our nation and in our world?"

Yes. But to do so we must get busy drilling. We must embark on our own personal transformation by saying, "I want to change. I want to grow. I want to excel, live a more productive life, and be more effective as a believer." We must draw deeply on the treasures of wisdom stored up in Christ and extract them like oil from a well.

## TAPPING INTO WISDOM'S TREASURES

Once those treasures are pumped up out of our heart, we can use them for different purposes in our life. Just as oil is processed and used for gasoline in one place and manufacturing in another, we can process God's wisdom and benefit from it in all kinds of wonderful ways. We can use it at home, at work, in our relationships, in our finances—everywhere!

We can become so fruitful and productive in every area of our lives that we attract the attention of people around us who don't know Jesus. They'll start watching us and asking how we're having so much success. They'll want to know Who we know. Then we can tell them and then they'll get to know Him too.

This has always been God's plan for the church. But it hasn't yet been fully carried out because, to a great extent, the vast resources of wisdom He has made available to us in Christ are "still unexplored."[13]

Leaving resources unexplored is a waste! If you need proof of it, think about the expansion that's taken place in America over the past 200 years. It's developed in almost unimaginable ways. It's grown from a few struggling colonies huddled together on the east coast into a nation that stretches from the Atlantic to the Pacific and is arguably the most powerful in the world.

None of this would have happened, however, if America hadn't had any explorers. For it to become what it is today, somebody had to have a pioneer spirit. Somebody had to be willing to press through adversity and push

---
13 Colossians 2:3, Jordan's Translation

forward spiritually, mentally, emotionally, and physically. Somebody had to be willing to travel across this land and explore it.

If you've studied American history, you know that once the explorers did their part and opened various frontiers across this country, other people came along who had a different mindset. They just wanted to settle in and get comfortable. They reaped the benefits of their trailblazing predecessors, but instead of putting forth the same kind of effort, they just built museums commemorating the pioneers' achievements. They stocked the museums with historic memorabilia, gave guided tours, and sold fifty cent souvenirs for $15.

Although it's sad to say, it's the same way in the Church. There are pioneers and there are settlers. There are people who make things happen and people who just talk about what happened.

God is looking for more pioneers! He's looking for people who will explore the spiritual land they've been given. People who will dig a little deeper and go a little higher. People who will press forward into the "unexplored" riches of God's wisdom, lay hold of new ideas, get fresh direction from God, and discover what His will is for their lives.

## One Effective Way to Drill

"Well, that all sounds good on paper," you might say. "I like the idea of drilling, exploring, and tapping into all this wisdom God has stored up for me. But exactly how do I go about doing it?"

There are a number of ways, and we'll be talking about them throughout the remainder of this book. But way number one is this:

Tap into the wisdom of God by praying for it! Go boldly to His throne of grace in prayer and request the divine insight you need to deal wisely with the particular situations you are facing in your life. In other words, follow the instructions in James 1:5: "If any of you lacks wisdom, let him ask of God, who gives to all liberally and without reproach, and it will be given to him."

Notice that verse makes an absolute promise. It doesn't say God *might* give you the wisdom you need. It doesn't say *sometimes He'll give it and other times He won't*. It says God *will* give wisdom to those who request it. Jesus confirmed this. He said:

> Ask, and it will be given to you; seek, and you will find; knock, and it will be opened to you. For everyone who asks receives, and he who seeks finds, and to him who knocks it will be opened. (Luke 11:9-10)

Many Christians want wisdom. They wish for it. But they don't actually ask God to give it to them. They don't go knocking on His door. And if they do, they don't necessarily believe He will open it and grant their request. As a result, they end up disappointed because, according to the Bible, anybody who wants to receive wisdom from God must:

> …ask in faith, with no doubting, for he who doubts is like a wave of the sea driven and

tossed by the wind. For let not that man suppose that he will receive anything from the Lord; he is a double-minded man, unstable in all his ways. (James 1:6-8)

To tap into a gusher of God's wisdom always ask for it in faith. Be confident God will give it to you. Don't let the winds of adversity cause you to waver back and forth. Don't believe in one moment that God will answer your prayer and doubt it the next. Do what Jesus said in Mark 11:24: "Whatever things you ask when you pray, believe that you receive them, and you will have them."
One version of the Bible translates that verse like this: "...whatever you pray for and ask, believe you have got it and you shall have it."

Although that may sound like a contradiction, it's how faith works. Faith is always now. It believes it receives the moment it asks. Faith doesn't say, "Oh, I've asked God for wisdom but I haven't received it yet. I sure hope He gives it to me soon." No, faith says, "I made my request and God answered it. I believe I have what I asked for right now."

If you're not comfortable with such faith confessions, you may be thinking, *But I really don't know what to do about my situation. If I said I have God's wisdom about it, I'd be lying!*

On the contrary, if you said it in faith you'd be telling the truth. You'd be doing what Jesus commanded in Mark 11:22-23 when He said:

Have faith in God. For assuredly, I say to you,

whoever says to this mountain, "Be removed and be cast into the sea," and does not doubt in his heart, but believes that those things he says will be done, he will have whatever he says.

Ultimately, you're going to have what you say. So if you don't like what you have, then change what's coming out of your mouth. If you don't like running short of wisdom, declare that you have it. Even if you still feel as clueless as ever, forget your feelings and speak by faith. Use your mouth to affirm what you believe.

As I've already mentioned, that's what I do. When I don't have the insight to know what my next step is in a particular situation, I not only pray, I *say*. I declare by faith: "I know what to do. I know when to do it. I know how to do it. And I know with whom to do it."

That's one of the ways I drill!

## Not Just a One-Time Event

Here's something else I do when I want to tap into more of God's wisdom. I pray the prayers the Apostle Paul prayed for the early New Testament believers. Those prayers are especially powerful. They came forth by the inspiration of the Holy Spirit and are recorded in Scripture. Because they reflect the perfect will of God, they're prayers we can be confident He will answer.

One such prayer can be found in the first chapter of Colossians. It says:

> For this reason we also, since the day we heard it, do not cease to pray for you, and to ask that you may be filled with the knowledge of His will in all wisdom and spiritual understanding; that you may walk worthy of the Lord, fully pleasing Him, being fruitful in every good work and increasing in the knowledge of God; strengthened with all might, according to His glorious power, for all patience and longsuffering with joy; (vv. 9-11)

This is a wonderful example of how to ask God for wisdom. It's a prayer that's appropriate for us to pray for ourselves as individuals, for our church, or for other Christians anywhere in the world that the Lord might put on our heart. So let's examine it closely to see what we can learn from it.

Notice, first of all, the phrase *"we do not cease to pray for you"* (v. 9). This tells us that asking God for wisdom isn't a one-time event. It needs to be done on an on-going basis. New challenges are always arising in our lives. We can't plan today for all the circumstances we will face tomorrow. Our future is full of unexpected trials and pressures and we need a constant stream of God's wisdom to bring us through each one of them in triumph.

What's more, no matter how much we know about God and His plan, there's always more to learn. God always has fresh insights to give us. He wants to continually reveal to us more of Himself, His perspective, and His principles so we can continually grow.

The Apostle Paul knew this. He knew the believers he was praying for would always need more wisdom. That's why he never ceased to ask God to give it to them. We should do the same for ourselves! We should follow Paul's example and ask God (without ceasing!) that we may be "filled with the knowledge of His will in all wisdom and spiritual understanding."

When you're filled with the knowledge of God's will, you're able to follow His plan and grasp His purpose for your life. You have His insight into any situation that arises. You can see about it what God sees and know what He wants you to do.

When you're filled with spiritual wisdom and understanding, He can direct you and order your steps. He can correct you when necessary. He can show you how to apply His principles so that in your daily lifestyle "you may walk worthy of the Lord, fully pleasing Him, being fruitful in every good work" (v. 10).

Being fruitful and productive in life, although it's what we all want, isn't as easy as it sounds. There are challenges we have to conquer and an adversary to overcome. On one hand, we have to contend with our lazy old flesh. On the other hand, we have to deal with the devil. Both present us with difficulties in life that we have to press through.

Say, for instance, you need additional education to excel in your profession. You can't get that education by just sitting in a classroom looking at your cell phone. You can't learn what you need to know if you're constantly checking social media and text messaging when the lessons are being taught.

No, whether you like it or not, you have to listen to what the professors are saying. You have to read the books and do the assignments. Otherwise, you won't have the knowledge necessary to pass the tests. And if you don't pass the tests, you won't get the grades you need to graduate.

That's the way it is in every area of life. Whether in school or on the job, in your marriage or as a parent, to walk worthy of God and be fruitful in your endeavors, you'll have to do some things that are not your cup of tea. You'll have to be longsuffering enough to endure some unpleasantness, to persevere through the hard times and hang tough until you have accomplished your goal.

Although it's sad to say, a lot of Christians don't have the inner strength to do this. Their resolve is weak because they're so focused on the difficulties and pressures they're experiencing today, they forget about tomorrow. They let their emotions take over and they give up and quit. "I don't want to do this!" they say.

To avoid making that mistake, pray like Paul prayed. Drill down into the wisdom of God and be "strengthened with all might, according to His glorious power, for all patience and longsuffering with joy" (v. 11).

God's wisdom will give you a vision for your future. It will help you look past the present moment. It will enable you to see that if you persevere through the difficulties you'll receive a reward. If you apply yourself now, and press through to the finish line, you'll win the race. You'll receive the prize. You'll reap the benefits that come from endurance and enjoy a blessed and fruitful life.

## Be Ready for the Fork in the Road

In addition to the prayer in the first chapter of Colossians, there's one more New Testament prayer I want to mention that can help you learn to pray effectively for wisdom. It's found in Philippians chapter 1 where Paul penned these words:

> And this I pray, that your love may abound still more and more in knowledge and all discernment, that you may approve the things that are excellent, that you may be sincere and without offense till the day of Christ, being filled with the fruits of righteousness which are by Jesus Christ, to the glory and praise of God. (vv. 9-11)

Notice those verses connect love with wisdom. Why? Because the two go hand-in-hand. We have poor judgment when we're not walking in love. We make bad choices when we're frustrated and angry with people.

Have you ever been upset with somebody and reacted by making a hasty decision? Have you ever gotten fed up with a situation and behaved in an ugly way? If so, you know how unwise it can be.

When your emotions are inflamed and you're feeling pressured to make a decision, it's better to pull back spiritually and mentally, to say, "I'm going to stop right now and press into God. I'm not going act foolishly and head down a path that will lead to destruction. I'm going to ask God to help me walk in love."

The Amplified Bible says love will enable you to "sense what is vital, and approve and prize what is excellent and of real value [recognizing the highest and the best, and distinguishing the moral differences]" (v. 9). It will enable you, as William Barclay puts it, "to decide between the different courses of action which present themselves to you."[14]

Knowing what course of action to choose is important! It can make all the difference because again and again in life you're going to come to vital forks in the road. What are you going to do when that happens?

Well, as Yogi Berra used to say, "When you come to a fork in the road, take it." But before you do, tap into the wisdom of God and find out which path to take, which way to go. Pray for Him to cause your love to abound and ask Him for more knowledge and all discernment.

He'll give you all you need. He'll direct you and show you the path that will cause you to be fruitful in everything you do.

---

14  William Barclay, The New Testament, A New Translation, Volume Two, (New York: Collins), 140

## TAPPING INTO WISDOM'S TREASURES

### *Confession*

Father, You said in Your Word that if I ask You for wisdom, You will give it to me liberally. So I ask You to give me wisdom regarding _____. I thank You for hearing me and answering my request. I believe I receive the wisdom I need. I declare by faith that I have it. God has given it to me and it is mine now, in Jesus Name.

### *Summary Questions*

1. What excites you about the spiritual account God has provided for you in Christ? What do you want to know about it?

2. Can you be confident it's God's will for you to have His wisdom? Does the fact that Colossians 2:3 refers to His wisdom as "hidden" make you wonder if you can have it? Why or why not?

3. Why do we as believers sometimes experience a shortage of divine wisdom?

4. What's one thing we can we do to address this shortage?

5. In what specific areas of your life would you like to have more divine wisdom? How do you think that wisdom could help you and make you more fruitful in those areas?

# Chapter 3
## Like a Tree by the Water

*Blessed is the man who trusts in the LORD, and whose hope is the LORD. For he shall be like a tree planted by the waters, which spreads out its roots by the river, and will not fear when heat comes; but its leaf will be green, and will not be anxious in the year of drought, nor will cease from yielding fruit.*
Jeremiah 17:7-8

Here in Las Vegas we can easily picture what Jeremiah meant when he referred to "the year of drought." We experience it pretty much every year. Our entire average annual rainfall amounts to about four inches, so for us drought isn't the exception, it's the rule.

Unlike the land Jeremiah wrote about, however, in

# TAPPING INTO WISDOM'S TREASURES

our little corner of Nevada we don't have any rivers flowing through town where trees can spread out their roots. We just have craggy creek beds we call "washes." On occasion, a cloudburst will flood them with water and they'll briefly become rivers. But before long the water is gone and they're nothing but dried up gulches again.

Still, the washes manage to illustrate Jeremiah's point. They always have more vegetation growing in them than other desert areas do. Why? Because the water that flows through them, limited as it may be, soaks into the soil and becomes an underground source of moisture. The roots of the plants tunnel down and tap into it, and it provides them with life.

That's a perfect picture of what we as believers can do. As we send our roots down into the wisdom of God, we can flourish in the midst of even the most challenging circumstances.

In the natural, everything around us might be dry and desolate. Leaves might be falling. Things might be dying. But because we're tapping into the wisdom that's ours in Christ, our lives will look like a well-watered garden. Right in the middle of a drought-ridden world, we'll bear abundant fruit.

It's no wonder Proverbs 4:7 says, "Wisdom is the principal thing; therefore get wisdom. And in all your getting, get understanding." God's wisdom is like water in a desert. It's absolutely essential to life, and in the spiritually drought-ridden climate of this world we can't get as much as we need by just sitting around wishing for it. We have

*Like a Tree by the Water*

to go after it. We have to *get it with all our getting*. Like a tree growing in a dried up wash, we have to sink our taproot down deep.

As we saw in the previous chapter, the number one way we do this is by praying. We simply ask God for wisdom and receive it by faith. In this chapter we'll focus on the second way of accessing the limitless wisdom that's ours in Christ: Meditating on and confessing God's Word.

Psalm 1 is one of many passages in the Bible that talks about just how powerful this method of connecting with God's wisdom can be. It says:

> Blessed is the man who walks not in the counsel of the ungodly, nor stands in the path of sinners, nor sits in the seat of the scornful; but his delight is in the law of the LORD, and in His law he meditates day and night. He shall be like a tree planted by the rivers of water, that brings forth its fruit in its season, whose leaf also shall not wither; and whatever he does shall prosper. (vv. 1-3)

Notice this passage begins by telling us what the blessed man—the man who lives in a well-watered oasis of God's manifest goodness—does not do. He doesn't listen to the world's counsel and fall prey to the sinners' way of thinking. He isn't scornful and skeptical of God's Word and His ways. On the contrary...

- His delight and desire are in the law of the Lord, and on His law (the precepts, the instructions, the teachings of God) he habitually meditates (ponders and studies) by day and by night. (v. 1, AMP)

- [His] greatest pleasure is in the law of the Lord so that day and night he recites this law to himself. (Norlie)

- He finds joy in the eternal's law, pouring over it day and night. (Moffatt Translation)

- In His law does he talk with himself day and night. (Rotherham's Emphasized Bible)

The *law of the Lord* as it's used in this scripture simply refers to the first part of the Old Testament. It was the only portion of the Bible that existed when Psalm 1 was written. Today we have more of the Word available to us. As New Covenant believers, we have all of the Old Testament and the New Testament as well.

That means we have an edge on the man in Psalm 1! We have the entire written Word of God. And because it all contains His wisdom, when we meditate on it, it ministers life to us. Our leaves turn green, so to speak. Areas of our lives that were once withered and barren perk up and become productive.

Think about a house plant that hasn't been watered for a while. The foliage might be drooping and the stalks might look hopelessly bent. But if you water it, 30 minutes later it will be standing up straight again. It will be revived and thriving.

That's what the water of God's Word does for us as

Christians. It revives us when we're drooping. As we soak ourselves in it by meditating on it day and night, it comes alive in us by the power of the Holy Spirit. It infuses us with what we need to stand up straight and thrive!

### God's Word is the Secret to Our Success

One person who would be quick to confirm this is the Old Testament leader, Joshua. When he was facing the enormous task of leading the Israelites into the Promised Land he needed wisdom in a big way. So God told him how to get it. After giving him some words of encouragement and commanding him not to be afraid, He said:

> This Book of the Law shall not depart from your mouth, but you shall meditate in it day and night, that you may observe to do according to all that is written in it. For then you will make your way prosperous, and then you will have good success.

Everybody would like to prosper and have good success. Everyone would like to "deal wisely," as the Amplified Bible puts it, because when we're wise in our dealings, we make the right choices. We get on the right path and go in the right direction. We find God's plan for our lives and, as a result, we keep increasing, advancing, and walking in victory.

That's the way we all want to live—and, praise God, we can do it! We can get the same results Joshua did by meditating on God's Word, by keeping it in our mouths day and night.

What does our mouth have to do with it? Everything! The primary definition of the word *meditate* is *to speak, to utter, or to talk to yourself.* Therefore, when we're meditating on God's Word, we're not just thinking about it in silence. We're actually talking to ourselves about it.

"But Pastor David," you might say, "I like talking to other people. I'm not comfortable talking to myself!"

Yes, you are. You do it all the time. Sometimes you look in the mirror and you talk to yourself about what you wish you did or didn't see there. Sometimes you talk to yourself about the circumstances you're facing. If you're walking through the house in the dark and you stub your toe, you'll talk to yourself!

What's more, you believe what you're saying. Someone else can tell you something and you can reject it. You can decide it's not true, choose to disregard it, and it won't have any real effect on you. Even if you do accept what somebody else says, it won't really have much impact on your life until you assimilate it in your own heart and mind, repeat it yourself, and make it your own. Only then will you really believe it.

What you say to yourself carries more weight in your own mind than anything anybody else can ever say. Therefore, you are the most important person you're talking to! So here's the big question: What are you saying to yourself?

According to Joshua 1:8, if you want to prosper and have good success, you'll be talking to yourself about the

Word of God. You won't just be talking about it once in a while, either. You'll be doing it day and night. Since night comes when the day ends, and day comes when the night ends, on a continual, consistent basis, you'll be speaking God's Word and agreeing with what He says about you.

You don't have to do this at the top of your lungs. To meditate literally means *to say again and again in a low tone; or to sing and to celebrate.* So you can do it very effectively by just muttering to yourself in whispers no one else can hear. You can also add melody to the scriptures you're pondering and rejoice over them in song.

## A Divine Progression

The purpose of such meditation isn't just to gain knowledge for knowledge's sake. It's not just so you'll know something someone else doesn't know. The reason you want to keep God's Word in your heart and in your mouth day and night is so you can "observe to do according to all that is written in it."

Meditation is part of a divine progression. As you meditate on the Word, your heart and your mind are enlightened. You come to understand some things you didn't understand before. The Holy Spirit clarifies what God is saying to you in the Scriptures. He graces you to see clearly, from God's perspective, exactly what you need to do. Then by acting on what He shows you, "you will make your way prosperous."

Notice, it's not just God who makes your way

prosperous. Your prosperity is determined by what *you* do. Your success comes when you act on what you see in the Scriptures by following through and obeying what the Holy Spirit has taught you through them. This is how you deal wisely, make wise choices, find God's direction, and fulfill His will for your life.

In the end, fulfilling God's will for your life is all that really matters. When you're in His perfect will, everything you put your hand to prospers because you're following His divine guidance system. You're in the right place at the right time doing the right thing with the right people.

The safest and the most blessed place for any believer to be is always in the will of God. But many Christians stop short of it by neglecting to act on the Word. Even though they know what it says and their eyes are opened to the truth, they don't follow through with obedience. They have the idea that just because they know and can quote the Bible everything is going to be all right.

James 1:22 warns us about this delusion. It says, "Be doers of the word, and not hearers only, deceiving yourselves."

"Well, I try to be a doer," somebody might say. "I have a few special scriptures I act on every day."

That may be fine as far as it goes, but it doesn't go far enough. God didn't say we should just take our favorite scriptures and obey them. He said, "Observe to do *all* that is written" in the Word of God.

Although there's nothing wrong with having verses you particularly enjoy, verses that really minister to you, beware of focusing on only certain portions of the Bible and ignoring the rest. Receive from God's Word all that the Holy Spirit is saying to you through it—whether He's ministering to you God's promises of blessing, instruction in righteousness, or correction.

I realize things like correction might not sound like much fun, but that doesn't matter. All of God's Word is vital. As you focus on it and meditate on it, it causes your faith to grow and develop. It sharpens your spiritual vision and keeps your perspective on target. When you allow the Word to correct you, you get better at what you're called to do. You're able to fulfill your purpose in life and stay on track to your destiny.

## Set Your Course and Don't Get Distracted

I know from personal experience how true this is. If I hadn't let God's Word instruct and correct me about how to walk out my ministry, I would have gotten off track long ago, because ever since I accepted God's call, people have been trying to involve me in things that would distract me. This started back when I was in Bible college. Well-meaning believers kept approaching me with business ideas and saying, "If you'd just do this, you could support yourself in ministry." Their suggestions seemed logical. They made mental sense and could easily have appealed to my normal, human desire for financial security. Yet they didn't sit right with me. I didn't believe God wanted me to do those things.

Why? Because in 1 Corinthians 9:14 He said, "Those

who preach the gospel should live from the gospel." And in 2 Timothy 2:3, He said to a young minister, "As Christ's soldier, do not let yourself become tied up in the affairs of this life, for then you cannot satisfy the one who has enlisted you in his army."[15]

Those scriptures were God's wisdom to me. I was committed to acting on what the Holy Spirit had said to me through them. So, even in my early years of ministry when my wife and I had to believe God for every dime, I chose not to involve myself in business.

The opportunities never stop presenting themselves, though. Even now people sometimes say to me, "Pastor, if you would take advantage of this business opportunity, it would be a financial blessing to you. You could be more prosperous and be a greater blessing to the church." But I don't have to fast for a week and pray about those ideas. I don't have to ask God if it's His will for me to act on them. I set my course many years ago. I know what God's plan is for me because God opened my eyes and gave me understanding. Through His Word, He showed me that if I didn't stay focused I'd end up using my time, my mind, and my energies on things God hasn't called me to do. Those things might be fine for others. But I have to stay on the path God has prepared for me.

I've become increasingly grateful over the years for the wisdom God has given me in this area because I've seen many ministers get distracted from their purpose. I've seen them involve themselves in business and forget

---

[15] NLT

about the ministry—sometimes even leave it altogether—because they were making money doing something else. I understand how that happens. If I didn't have insight about it from God it could have happened to me too. I could have been pulled in a lot of different directions.

The same is true for you. Regardless of your vocation, you need the wisdom of God. When you know what He's called you to do, you can avoid unprofitable distractions. You can follow the plan He has laid out for you with a spirit of faith and confidence. You can stay on track by saying, "No. I'm not going to be drawn off course by anything. I'm going to stick with the will of God for my life!"

"Well," somebody might say, "I'd like to do that but I can't hear from the Lord as clearly as you do." The Bible says you can. It says, "As many as are led by the Spirit of God, these are sons of God."[16] In other words, you and every other believer can have the Holy Spirit's direction for your life. You can know God's will, follow His plan for you, and fulfill your destiny. As you continually meditate on the Scriptures, you can receive revelation from God about exactly what you need to do because:

- The entrance of His words gives light; it gives understanding to the simple. (Ps. 119:130)

- His word is a lamp to your feet and a light to your path. (Ps. 119:105)

- The word of God is living and powerful, and sharper than any two-edged sword, piercing

---
16 Romans 8:14

even to the division of soul and spirit. (Heb. 4:12)

Notice that last verse refers to dividing your soul from your spirit. Although you may not have realized it, those are two very different things. Your soul includes your natural mental reasoning and your emotions. Your spirit is the inner part of you, the real you that was born again when you received Jesus as the Lord of your life.

When you're facing a choice or decision, you don't want to just rely on your natural reasoning or the emotions that are churning in your soul. They're limited and fallible. They will lie to you and steer you in the wrong direction when you're trying to discern what to do and which way to go.

If you let your soul direct you and you just try to figure things out with your head, you'll get confused. You'll think you're doing what's wise, but then your decision won't produce the results you thought it would and you'll wind up frustrated and upset.

The Word of God can help you avoid this frustration. As you meditate on it, it will divide your soul from your spirit. It will help you make a right decision that's not based on mental reasoning or emotion, but on the will of God.

This doesn't mean, of course, that you should never use your mind. Your mind is important! You'll need to engage it in order to accomplish what God leads you to do. The key is to make sure your mind is following the direction set by your spirit, the direction that's been revealed to you by the Holy Spirit speaking to you through God's Word.

Then, no matter what's going on around you, you'll be able to stick to God's plan and His will for your life. You won't be pushed off course by your natural senses because you'll have a perception that goes beyond them. You'll have a vision that outweighs the pull of your soul, a vision so big your mind can't even wrap around it.

As you look at that vision by faith, you'll see your future like God sees it. You'll hear the Holy Spirit say, "This is the way. This is the will of God. Walk in it!" And you'll be able to say in response, "Yes! With God I can!"

### Make Sure the Mountain Hears Your Voice

I'm not suggesting that once you're in the will of God you won't encounter any challenges. I'm not saying that discovering His plan for your success will enable you to breeze down life's highway without any problems. On the contrary, you'll always have plenty of obstacles to overcome.

The devil will see to that. He'll always be trying to stop you from running your race and fulfilling your destiny. He'll always put seemingly insurmountable mountains in front of you and throw hindrances in your way. That's why the Bible says things like, "Many are the afflictions of the righteous, but the LORD delivers him out of them all,"[17] and "In the world you will have tribulation; but be of good cheer, I have overcome the world."[18]

Trouble is an inevitable part of life. But if you'll

---

17  Psalm 34:19
18  John 16:33

meditate on the Word, when trouble comes you'll be equipped to overcome it. You'll be ready and able to triumph by acting on what Jesus said in Mark 11:23:

> Assuredly, I say to you, whoever says to this mountain, "Be removed and be cast into the sea," and does not doubt in his heart, but believes that those things he says will be done, he will have whatever he says.

Although meditation primarily means talking to yourself, according to this verse, when you find a mountain standing in your way you go a step further. You speak the Word to the mountain! You talk to the obstacle or the adversity that is telling you that you can't do what God has given you a vision to do. You tell it what God's Word says and command it to be gone.

This is what Jesus instructed all of us as His disciples to do. He didn't tell us to go around the mountain. He didn't say put your head in the sand and hope the mountain goes away. He said, "Confront it. Speak to it. Tell it to be removed."

The devil will try to make you feel like you can't obey those instructions. He'll try to convince you you're not qualified to declare God's Word with authority, that although others might be, you aren't. But the devil is a liar. According to Jesus, "whosoever" can speak to mountains. Anybody can do it.

To be as effective at it as you want to be you may have to make some adjustments in your life. But with the wisdom you get from the Word of God, you'll be able to make those adjustments. You'll be able to look at things from God's perspective and see past the mountain to what's on the other side. Instead of being afraid to face the mountain, you'll have the boldness to deal with it. You'll have faith to believe that when you tell the mountain to move, it *will* move.

God's Word can do mighty things for you! It's a vast and inexhaustible reservoir of His wisdom. So sink your roots down deep into it. As the Holy Spirit quickens specific scriptures to you, think about them and talk to yourself about them.

Follow the example of Mary, the mother of Jesus. When she heard the things the angel said to her about the birth of the Savior, she "pondered them in her heart."[19] She meditated on the Word of God that had been spoken to her. Then she said, "Let it be to me according to your word."[20]

God wants us all to do what Mary did. He wants us to agree with His Word and confess it boldly by faith!

*Confess* means *to say the same thing.* Therefore when you confess God's Word you're saying the same thing He says about you and your life. Why is that important? Because according to the Bible, you will have what you say—for better or for worse. As Proverbs 18:21 puts it, "Death and life are in the power of the tongue, and those who love it will eat its fruit."

Today you're eating the fruit of what you've said in days gone by. If you don't like that fruit, you can change it

---
19 Luke 2:19
20 Luke 1:38

## TAPPING INTO WISDOM'S TREASURES

by saying something different. You can speak God's Word to the mountain that's standing in your way. You can speak out the vision God has given you and the promises He has made alive in your heart.

As you speak God's words over your life, God will bring them to pass. His vision for you will become a reality in your life. Right in the middle of the desert, you'll become like a tree planted by the rivers of water. You'll prosper and have good success.

## *Confession*

I delight in God's Word because His Word is His wisdom. As I meditate on it and confess it, the Holy Spirit enlightens my understanding and teaches me what to do. The entrance of God's Word into my heart gives me light. It reveals to me God's will for my life. It helps me divide between soul and spirit so I can be led, not by my natural mind and emotions, but by God's Spirit. As I keep God's Word in my heart and in my mouth, and do what the Holy Spirit teaches me through the Word I should do, I am like a tree planted by rivers of water. I bear abundant fruit and everything I do prospers!

## *Summary Questions*

1. Describe how the Word of God affects your life like water in the desert.

2. What does the word meditate mean to you?

3. What causes many believers to stop short of God's perfect will?

4. Why is it important for you to be able to divide between soul and spirit?

5. What can you do about the mountains that try to stand in the way of God's vision for your life?

# Chapter 4
## Winning the Tug-O-War

*And they were all filled with the Holy Spirit and began to speak with other tongues, as the Spirit gave them utterance.*

Acts 2:4

No group of Christians in history has ever needed wisdom more than the 120 believers who gathered in the upper room in the first chapter of Acts. They had just received the Great Commission. They'd been called by the Lord Jesus Himself to spread the Gospel to the ends of the earth.

And they had no idea how to go about it.

Jesus had ascended to heaven so He wasn't physically present anymore to show them what to do, and they didn't yet have a written New Testament to instruct them. They couldn't open their Bible like we do and study Paul's

# TAPPING INTO WISDOM'S TREASURES

revelations about the riches of their inheritance in Christ. They couldn't read and meditate on verses about how Jesus "...became for us wisdom from God," and "In [Him] are hid all the treasures of wisdom and knowledge."[21]

Although they'd essentially been entrusted with the future of the Church, they had no church-planting books to advise them. They had no church-growth conferences to attend. The only thing they knew to do was to follow the instructions Jesus had given them just before He'd ascended to heaven.

"Don't leave Jerusalem," He said. "But wait for the Promise of the Father. For you shall be baptized with the Holy Spirit not many days from now. And you shall receive power when the Holy Spirit has come upon you; and you shall be witnesses to Me in Jerusalem, and in all Judea and Samaria, and to the end of the earth."[22]

Armed with this promise, the early believers gathered in Jerusalem to pray; and, as the second chapter of Acts records:

> When the Day of Pentecost had fully come, they were all with one accord in one place. And suddenly there came a sound from heaven, as of a rushing mighty wind, and it filled the whole house where they were sitting. Then there appeared to them divided tongues, as of fire, and one sat upon each of them. And they were all filled with the Holy Spirit and began

---
21 1 Corinthians 1:30, Colossians 2:3
22 Acts 1:5, 8

to speak with other tongues, as the Spirit gave them utterance. And there were dwelling in Jerusalem Jews, devout men, from every nation under heaven. And when this sound occurred, the multitude came together, and were confused, because everyone heard them speak in his own language. Then they were all amazed and marveled... (Acts 2:2-7)

Those verses are some of the most thrilling in the Bible. If you're a Spirit-filled believer, you've probably read them many times. But there's one thing they reveal you may not have seriously considered. They tell us that at a time when the Church most needed divine wisdom, understanding, direction, and revelation, the very first gift the Holy Spirit provided was the ability to speak in other tongues.

Sometimes I think modern day Christians overlook this. When we read about the first Pentecostal outpouring, we tend to think of speaking in tongues as simply a sign and wonder. We view it primarily as a supernatural attraction given by God to get the attention of the crowds on the streets of Jerusalem that day.

Certainly there's nothing wrong with this perspective. The tongues spoken in Acts 2 did indeed serve as a supernatural sign. And quite often they serve the same purpose today. I can testify of it myself.

I remember one church service, for instance, when I prayed in tongues and afterward I was approached by a woman who knew about six different languages. She said,

"Pastor, you spoke in this particular language and this is what you said." I hadn't understood the words I'd prayed but she understood them perfectly and they blessed her.

But that's not all there is to speaking and praying in tongues. It's not just a gift given to preachers for the purpose of ministry and evangelism. It's an ability God has made available to every believer for the purpose of helping us live in victory in our everyday lives. As Peter said in Acts 2:39 to the multitudes who marveled at the manifestation of this wonderful gift, "The promise is to you and to your children, and to all who are afar off, as many as the Lord our God will call."

In this chapter, we will focus on praying in other tongues (or "praying in the spirit" as some scriptures refer to it) because it provides us with a third way to tap into our divine resources. Like prayer, meditation and confession of God's Word, speaking in tongues helps us to drill down into the wisdom that belongs to us in Christ.

## Divine Mysteries and Secrets

"But Pastor David," you might say, "praying in tongues involves saying words I don't understand. How could that have anything to do with wisdom? How could it possibly help me make good choices and decisions about the practical issues of life?"

According to the New Testament, it can help you in a number of different ways.

First of all, by praying in tongues you can pray about

things that are hidden from your natural understanding. You can talk to God about aspects of His will for you that haven't yet been revealed. You can also speak to Him about future events you aren't yet aware of that will eventually affect your life.

First Corinthians 14:2 explains it this way: "He who speaks in a tongue does not speak to men but to God, for no one understands him; however, in the spirit he speaks mysteries."[23] Being able to pray about *mysteries* (or *divine secrets* and *secret truths,* as various translations call them) gives you a tremendous advantage. It takes the limits off your prayer life. It enables you to pray not just according to what you know, but according to the infinite wisdom and knowledge of God.

Another benefit of praying in tongues is found in 1 Corinthians 14:4. There, the Apostle Paul said, "He who speaks in a tongue edifies himself." The word *edify* means *to build up*. It can be used to refer to the construction of a house or some other natural structure. It also speaks of charging something up, like you might charge a battery.

If you have a cell phone (and who doesn't these days?) you're well acquainted with this concept. You know what happens after you use your cell phone all day. The battery gets low and you have to plug it into a power source to recharge it. Otherwise, the phone will stop working.

Spiritually, much the same thing is true. To keep your spiritual communication systems working properly, you have to plug into the power source of the Holy Spirit.

---
23  1 Corinthians 14:2

## TAPPING INTO WISDOM'S TREASURES

You have to regularly recharge your inner man so that you're continually able to hear from God.

Hearing from God is vital! That's why Jude 1:20 says to build yourself up on your most holy faith, praying in the Holy Spirit. You don't want to find yourself in the middle of some challenging circumstance and suddenly realize your spiritual battery is low. You don't want to find yourself saying, like the guy on the television commercial, "Can you hear me now?" You want to have confidence every day that your connection with God is strong. You want your spirit to be charged up so you're quick to pick up on His signals.

Think again about your cell phone. If you don't plug it into the power source tonight, tomorrow you might miss a very important call. Somebody you don't even know might try to reach you with news that could change your life. Their call might be more important than any call you've received all year. But it won't get through to you if your cell phone battery isn't charged.

By the same token, if you don't charge up your spirit regularly, God will be trying to get a message to you but won't be able to receive it. You'll miss out on His call. You'll fail to pick up on the wisdom He's endeavoring to give you about the circumstances you're facing and you'll wind up having to make decisions based on your own natural reasoning and emotions. You don't ever want to be in that situation—and you don't have to be! You can keep yourself charged up spiritually. You can stay continually tuned into God's frequency. You can hear from Him anytime of the day or night and receive all the wisdom you need.

That wisdom already belongs to you because God has made it to abound toward you in Christ.[24] It's available to you in abundance to help you live your life to the fullest. Praying in other tongues will simply help you access it. It will help keep your spiritual battery strong so that when God speaks you'll always be able to say to Him, "Yes, I can hear You now!"

## Protection from Deception

Over the years, I've seen the benefits of praying in other tongues not only in my own life but in the lives of many other believers as well. I know of several businessmen, for instance, who became tremendously successful, in part, because they prayed in the Spirit over their financial affairs.

One of them made his money in real estate, buying and developing properties. He started out with only $500 to invest. But over time he became a multimillionaire. Because he was very generous in giving to the work of the Lord, as his wealth increased, his offerings did too. I remember hearing about one particular offering he gave that was a million dollars.

Personally, I think having a million dollars cash to give away is significant. So I found it very interesting when I heard him talk about how he became prosperous enough to do it. He said the secret to his success was that he'd trained himself to hear the voice of the Holy Spirit in his heart. He explained that every morning for months on end, he listened to a scriptural message on the subject by a trusted minister.

---
24  Ephesians 1:7-8

## TAPPING INTO WISDOM'S TREASURES

He also spent time worshipping and fellowshipping with God, meditating on His Word, and praying in tongues. As a result, his spiritual hearing became very keen.

When he attended board meetings, he was able to listen not just to the natural conversations going on around him but also to what God was saying in his spirit. Sometimes his natural mind would tell him, "This is a great opportunity! You ought to invest in this!" But his heart would say, "Don't do it." The more he learned to hear and follow the leading in his heart, the more successful he became.

Another wealthy investor I heard about did much the same thing. When people would come to him and ask him to finance various business opportunities, he'd say, "Let me pray about it." Then he'd spend a day (or two or three) praying and waiting on God. When he got his answer he would tell them yes or no. Because he only said yes when the Lord gave him the go-ahead, his investments consistently prospered.

"Well," you might say, "I've heard about so-called prophets who claimed they had a word from God and went around prophesying to people about making certain investments. Everybody who listened to them lost money!"

I've heard such stories too. They always remind me that God never intended for us to depend on other people for guidance, even if those people are supposedly prophets. Each one of us is responsible to hear what God is saying in our own heart. If we'll do our part by meditating on His Word and praying in other tongues (both are necessary for a balanced spiritual life) the Holy Spirit will help us in our decision making.

He'll protect us from selfish, designing people who try to manipulate or control us. He'll keep us from being misled by those who, either intentionally or unintentionally, would deceive us or take advantage of us in some way. As we pay attention to the Holy Spirit's still, small voice on the inside of us, He will give us the discernment we need. He'll show us what to do, when to do it, how to do it, and with whom to do it, so that we don't get shipwrecked by somebody else's unwise counsel.

How can you be certain this kind of protection is actually available to you? Because the Apostle John wrote in the New Testament:

> You have an anointing from the Holy One, and you know all things...I have written to you concerning those who try to deceive you. But the anointing which you have received from Him abides in you, and you do not need that anyone teach you; but as the same anointing teaches you concerning all things, and is true, and is not a lie, and just as it has taught you, you will abide in Him. (1 John 2:20, 26-27)

Those verses aren't saying that because we as individual believers have the Holy Spirit to teach us we don't need any Bible teachers. If that were true, the Head of the Church, the Lord Jesus Christ, would not have given "some to be apostles, some prophets, some evangelists, and some pastors and teachers, for the equipping of the saints for the work of ministry, for the edifying of the body of Christ."[25]

Jesus wouldn't call and anoint teachers if we didn't need to be taught. So it's important to keep these verses in context. When the Apostle John said, "You need not that anyone should teach you," He was referring to the confusion that was being caused by deceptive people who had infiltrated the Church. He was simply saying that as believers we have a way to protect ourselves from being fooled by such individuals. We don't have to allow ourselves to be led astray because we "know all things."

Obviously, with your natural understanding, you don't know all things. But in Christ are hidden all the treasures of wisdom and knowledge; and because you're in Him that knowledge can be revealed to you by the Holy Spirit who lives inside you. You can tap into it as you draw on the anointing, or the "unction," as the King James Version of the Bible translates it, of the Holy Spirit.

If you don't utilize this unction by praying in tongues, you'll miss out on some of the wisdom that's available to you and you'll be more vulnerable to deceptive people. They'll have a better shot at seducing you into believing something that's not true and convincing you to follow a path that's not wholesome for your life. So, clearly, it's worth it to take the time to pray.

## With the Holy Spirit on Your Team

Romans 8:26-27 paints a remarkable picture of what

---
25 Ephesians 4:11-12

happens during this process of praying and speaking in other tongues. It says:

> The Spirit also *helps* in our *weaknesses*. For we do not know what we should pray for as we ought, but the Spirit Himself makes intercession for us with groanings which cannot be uttered. Now He who searches the hearts knows what the mind of the Spirit is, because He makes intercession for the saints according to the will of God.

Notice I italicized two words in that passage. The first one, *helps*, is translated from a compound Greek term that means *to take hold together with against*. The second word which is translated *weaknesses* refers to *an inability to produce results*. Used together, these words describe how the Holy Spirit takes hold together with us against whatever adversity or contrary circumstances we might face and empowers us to produce results we are unable to achieve on our own.

The description brings to mind the image of a tug-o-war. You probably played that game when you were kid so you know how it goes. You have two groups of people pulling on opposite ends of a rope with each group trying to drag the other toward their side. If the strength of the two groups is relatively equal, you have a stalemate. Everybody is straining and pulling with all their might and nobody is getting anywhere. But if you just add one more person to one end of the rope—it doesn't even have to be a really strong person—the group on that side will have what they need to pull the opposing team over the line. They'll have enough power to win the game.

The Holy Spirit is the extra Person on our side of the tug-o-war! He is our "strength," as Psalm 46:1 says, "A very present help in trouble." He takes hold with us and provides us with the help we need to live in victory. In areas where we are weak and unable to produce results in our life, He fortifies us with His strength so we can win.

One way He does this is by helping us when we pray. Because many times we don't know what to pray for, or how to pray most effectively, the Holy Spirit assists us by making intercession for us with *groanings which cannot be uttered.* According to Greek scholars, this phrase refers to prayers that cannot be articulated in our known or understood speech. In other words, it's talking about praying in tongues.

When you pray in other tongues, the Holy Spirit helps you to pray the perfect will of God. He enables you to speak, not just out of your own human reasoning, but with the very mind of Christ. Because you're speaking in a supernatural language, you may not understand what you're saying but God does. He hears and understands the prayers the Holy Spirit is helping you to pray, and He answers them.

What is the result?

Romans 8:28: "All things work together for good to those who love God, to those who are the called according to His purpose"!

This scripture is extremely popular among Christians, but it's often misunderstood. It's taken to mean that everything that happens is the will of God and it will automatically work out for the best. When you look at the verse in context, however, you can see it means something very different.

It's saying that when you pray in the Spirit, you pray the mind of God, therefore your prayers cause things to synergize and come together to work out His will in your life. Because with the Holy Spirit's help you've prayed the perfect prayers, God is taking care of business on your behalf. You have the witness in your heart that everything is going to be all right. He is working it all out for your good because you love Him, you are called according to His purpose, and you've taken some time to tap into His wisdom by praying in other tongues.

## Don't Let Tradition Rob You

Sadly, multitudes of Christians are robbed of these wonderful benefits of praying in tongues because they've been misguided by religious traditions. For instance, in the Pentecostal circles in which I grew up people thought they needed to have a "special feeling" to pray in the Spirit. They'd been taught they couldn't do it unless God's presence manifested in a spectacular way or the Holy Spirit moved on them in some extraordinary demonstration.

But that's a misconception. The truth is those of us who are Holy Spirit baptized believers can pray in tongues at will whenever we choose. We don't have to wait until we have a special feeling. We can simply follow the example of the Apostle Paul who said, "What is it then? I will pray with the spirit, and I will pray with the understanding also: I will sing with the spirit, and I will sing with the understanding also."[26]

"But how is that possible?" somebody might ask. "How can I pray at will in tongues if it's the Holy Spirit who is speaking?"

It's not the Holy Spirit who's speaking, it's you! You speak and He provides the words. That's what happened in Acts 2 on the day of Pentecost. "They were all filled with the Holy Spirit and [they] began to speak with other tongues, as the Spirit gave them utterance."[27]

People who don't understand this get all mixed up. They get the idea that the Holy Spirit will do all their praying for them. They think they can just assign their prayer projects to Him. But that's not scriptural. According to the Bible, the Holy Spirit's part is to supply the language. He does this by putting it in our spirit. Then we do our part by speaking it out.

The Apostle Paul put it this way: "If I pray in a tongue, my spirit prays."[28] Or as the Amplified Bible says, "My spirit [by the Holy Spirit within me] prays." In other words, when you're praying in the Spirit, your inner man is the one praying. The Holy Spirit gives you the ability, but your spirit has to release it. You have to open your mouth and pray.

Many years ago I learned that when ministering to

---

26  1 Corinthians 14:15

27  Verse 4

28  1 Corinthians 14:14

someone who wants to receive the baptism of the Holy Spirit, it's important to make this clear to them from the Scriptures. Otherwise they'll want to speak in tongues but they'll be hindered because they're expecting God to be responsible for every part of the process. They'll be waiting on Him to get hold of their tongue and make them speak. But He's not going to do it. They have to act by faith on the Word of God they've heard. They have to open their mouth and speak the words the Holy Spirit provides.

When I was going to Bible college, I rented a room from an elderly Pentecostal lady who had never understood this. At the time I met her, she'd only spoken in tongues one time in her life, forty years earlier when she had been initially filled with the Spirit. Think of it! She could have been praying in tongues every day for forty years but she was waiting to have some kind of special feeling (which, I suppose, she never felt).

I sat down with her and instructed her in what the Bible says about this. I told her she could pray in the spirit any day, anytime, anywhere. She could do it riding down the road in her car, working in her kitchen, or relaxing in her living room. "Wherever you are and whenever you choose," I said, "you can pray in other tongues."

Right now, I'm saying the same to you!

The Holy Spirit is living in you all the time and He doesn't take vacations. He doesn't just help you speak in tongues once or twice and then say, "Well, you're on your own from here." No, the Bible says, He never leaves or forsakes you. He is always there with you and in you, whether you feel Him or not.

This doesn't mean you shouldn't desire to feel the presence of God. Feeling His presence is a blessing! But you don't want to be dependent on feelings. You want to act on the Word and pray in the Spirit by faith even if you happen to be feeling as dry as day old toast. If you'll do that, as you release the Holy Spirit by praying in tongues, you'll often end up feeling God's presence in a very special way.

## Pray for Interpretation

Praying in other tongues is always beneficial, even when you don't understand what you're saying; but there are times when interpreting what you pray will produce even greater benefits. That's why Paul said this in 1 Corinthians 14:13: "Let him who speaks in a tongue pray that he may interpret."

Praying to interpret won't enable you to understand everything you say in tongues. That's not always necessary. But it will open the door for the Holy Spirit to help you interpret when it would be to your advantage to do so.

On some occasions He'll enable you to interpret so you can pray with your understanding about the mysteries you've been speaking in the Spirit. He'll reveal to you the divine secrets you've been talking about in tongues and enlighten your mind so that you can see and understand them to some degree. At other times, He'll grant you interpretation so you can speak or sing to yourself by the spirit of prophecy. Tongues and interpretation together equals prophecy, and prophecy serves to inspire, comfort, encourage, and build you up in the Lord.

The Holy Spirit will also give you interpretation in order to impart knowledge to you that would not be available to you any other way. Sometimes that knowledge concerns the future. As Jesus said, "When He, the Spirit of truth, has come, He will guide you into all truth; for He will not speak on His own authority, but whatever He hears He will speak; and He will tell you things to come."[29]

The Holy Spirit is your Helper. He's like a tour guide who will lead you in the path God has prepared for you. As you take the time to pray in tongues and ask for interpretation, He'll unveil the future to you so that you can know what direction you're to go. He'll bring forth the divine wisdom you need to make right choices and decisions. Then you can have the peaceful assurance in your heart that you're following God's plan for your life and everything is going to be all right!

---

29  John 16:13

TAPPING INTO WISDOM'S TREASURES

## *Confession*

The Holy Spirit is my Helper in prayer. He takes hold together with me and enables me to pray the perfect will of God for my life. By speaking out the spiritual languages He supplies to my spirit, I can pray mysteries and divine secrets. I can have the assurance in my heart that all things are working together for my good because I love the Lord, I am called according to His purpose, and I am taking time to pray in other tongues.

## *Summary Questions*

1. Why does praying mysteries in other tongues give you such an advantage?

2. 1 Corinthians 14:4 says, "He who speaks in an unknown tongue edifies himself." What does the word edify mean and how does it apply to praying in tongues?

3. Romans 8:26 says the Holy spirit "helps" us in our "weaknesses." What do those two words mean?

4. Do you need to have a special feeling in order to pray in tongues? Why or why not?

5. Why is it important to pray for the ability to interpret your tongues?

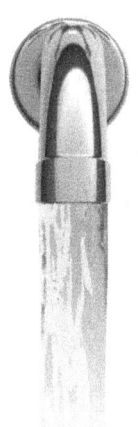

# Chapter 5
## Get Quiet and Listen

*And behold, the LORD passed by, and a great and strong wind tore into the mountains and broke the rocks in pieces before the LORD, but the LORD was not in the wind; and after the wind an earthquake, but the LORD was not in the earthquake; and after the earthquake a fire, but the LORD was not in the fire; and after the fire a still small voice. So it was, when Elijah heard it, that he wrapped his face in his mantle and went out and stood in the entrance of the cave.*

1 Kings 19:11-13

The day Elijah stood in the entrance of the cave on Mount Horeb he was desperate to hear from the Lord. His very life depended on it. With the murderous Queen Jezebel on his heels determined to kill him, he'd run until he was exhausted and had no place left to hide.

He no longer felt like the mighty prophet of faith and power he'd been when he called fire down from heaven and killed the prophets of Baal. Huddled in Horeb's cave, he just felt like a fugitive. Frightened and filled with despair, he'd even prayed he would die.

He couldn't see any other way out! Everything, it seemed, was working against him. When he cried out to God for guidance, the wind whipped around him until it split the rocks. Then the earth quaked. Then a fire raged.

And he didn't hear God's voice in any of it.

Ever been there?

Yes, you probably have.

So have I...and so has every other Christian.

We may not have been chased by a literal Jezebel or forced to hide in a cave. We may not have begged God to kill us (I don't recommend following that aspect of Elijah's example; it's not really scriptural) but we all know what it's like to go through tough times. We know how frustrating it can be when winds of adversity are blowing, situations are shaking and rattling, things are falling apart in ways we never expected, and in the midst of it all we can't seem to get any direction from the Lord.

What we want most at those times is for God to communicate with us in some dramatic way. We want Him to write us a personal message on a billboard beside the highway. Or yell instructions to us out of heaven with a booming, thunderous shout. But as most of us have discovered, the Lord rarely does those things.

Instead, He speaks on the inside of us in a still, small voice.

Over the years, I've noticed that for many believers this poses a problem because they're busy focusing on what's happening around them. They're searching for signs and seeking people to prophesy to them. And while they're looking for the spectacular, they miss the supernatural. They get discouraged and think God isn't talking to them at all.

It's a sad and sometimes tragic mistake. But it's not inevitable. You can avoid it simply by practicing the fourth way of tapping into the wisdom of God: Get quiet and listen to your spirit.

When it comes to hearing from heaven, your spirit is command central. It's the dwelling place of the Holy Spirit within you. It's the part of you that has the capacity to communicate with Him and find out what you need to know. As the Apostle Paul explained:

> No one knows the things of God except the Spirit of God. Now we have received, not the spirit of the world, but the Spirit who is from God, that we might know the things that have been freely given to us by God... The natural man does not receive the things of the Spirit of God, for they are foolishness to him; nor can he know them, because they are spiritually discerned. (1 Cor. 2:11-12, 14)

Look again at that last verse. It says the natural man

can't grasp the things of God; they have to be spiritually comprehended. You can know things in your spirit you'd never be able to figure out mentally. That's why people who try to understand the Bible with their intellect alone always end up confused. The Bible is not a mental book. It's a spiritual book. To truly grasp what it's saying you need the Holy Spirit to lead, guide, and teach you its meaning. And He can only do that by communicating with your spirit.

Proverbs 20:27 says it this way: "The spirit of man is the candle of the LORD, searching all the inward parts of the belly" (KJV).

Notice that verse doesn't say your *mind* or your *body* is the candle of the Lord. It says your *spirit* is His candle. In the days when Proverbs was written, candles were used as lamps to light up dark rooms. We don't use candles that way today, so these days we might say this: *The spirit of man is God's light bulb, illuminating all the inward parts of the belly.*

The word *belly* in this context doesn't mean *stomach*. (If it did, some of us would have more than others!) It's a spiritual term.[30] It speaks of the innermost part of a person or, as the New Testament calls it, "the hidden man of the heart."[31]

When God turns on the light bulb in your heart powerful things happen. You suddenly know what to do to overcome the challenge you've been facing. Confusion vanishes, and inspiration, revelation, and understanding

---

30 John 7:38: "He that believeth on me...out of his belly shall flow rivers of living water." (KJV)
31 1 Peter 3:4

come.[32] All at once you can say, as the psalmist did, "For You will light my lamp; the LORD my God will enlighten my darkness. For by You I can run against a troop, by my God I can leap over a wall."[33]

## Priming the Pump

*But if that's the case,* you might wonder, *why haven't I been running through any troops or leaping over any walls lately? Why am I still in the dark in some areas of my life?*

Well, it's certainly not because God hasn't turned on the light inside you. He did that the moment you were saved.[34] As we've seen in the previous chapters, all the light, wisdom, and knowledge of God are yours right now simply because you are in Christ. But to access those things, you must remember what Proverbs says:

Counsel in the heart of man is like deep water,
but a man of understanding will draw it out.
(v. 20:25)

The word *counsel* is defined in Strong's Concordance as *advice, plans, prudence, and purpose.* So that verse is actually saying: God's advice is in your heart. His plans and purposes are in your heart. You don't have to do your own thing and hope it will work out. You can get your directives straight from God. His divine counsel is on the inside of you in fathomless abundance. Like a bottomless well, it's

---
32  Job 32:8: "There is a spirit in man: and the inspiration of the Almighty giveth them understanding." (KJV)

33  Psalm 18:28-29

34  Ephesians 5:8 For you were once darkness, but now you are light in the Lord. Walk as children of light

really deep!

Sometimes the word *deep* can be used to refer to things that are complicated or hard to understand. I've known people who are called "deep" because when they talk nobody has a clue what they're saying. But that kind of depth isn't very helpful. I've found if I can't understand something, I can't apply it. And if I can't apply it, it's not going to help me. It's like muddy water in a lake. I can't see anything in it.

The deep counsel God puts within our spirit isn't like that. He doesn't give us muddy water. He makes things simple and easy to comprehend. He gives us directives that are so clear we can plainly see how to apply them—and when we do, things work out!

To discern those directives, though, we have to get quiet. We have to take time to listen to our spirit.

"But Pastor David," you might say, "I have so much going on in my life it's hard for me to do that. Every time I try, my mind gets noisy and instead of coming up with the deep waters of God's wisdom, I come up dry!"

I understand. The same thing used to happen to me sometimes when I was a kid and I tried to draw water out of the well on my uncle's farm. It was an old fashioned well with a bucket on it. Occasionally I'd let the bucket down on a chain, fill it with water, and haul it back up again. But most of the time I preferred to use the pump that was on the side of the well.

The only problem was when the pump was dry it wouldn't function properly. I could work it with all my might and no water would come up. So here's what I learned to do. I'd dip a little water out of the bucket and pour it over the top of the pump. As I was pouring, I'd push up and down on the handle. Then the well water would start to flow.

If you're of the Internet Generation and have never heard of this procedure, it's referred to as "priming the pump," and it's a natural illustration of what we as believers can do to solve a common spiritual problem. If we're having trouble hearing from the Lord, we can pour some spiritual water over ourselves. We can prime our spirit to tap into the wisdom of God.

How? By doing some of the things we've already discussed in this book. We can meditate and confess the Word, for instance. We can pray in other tongues. We can sing in the spirit and shout praises to God.

I've found it often helps me to get loud before I get quiet. It activates my spirit and helps me tune in to it.

I was thinking about this not long ago during one of our Sunday morning church services. Before I even started preaching, our congregation began to shout and give thanks and praise to the Lord. Although being loud in church makes some Christians nervous, it's thoroughly scriptural. Psalm 47:1 actually commands us to "shout unto God with the voice of triumph."

"Yeah, but what triumph were you shouting about?" somebody might say. "Your church service had barely gotten started!" I know it, but those of us who have faith in God don't have to wait until after a victory has been consummated in our lives before we can celebrate. We can

## TAPPING INTO WISDOM'S TREASURES

shout with joy in advance because we've read the Bible and we know what Jesus has done: He's already won the battle for us. He's whipped our enemy and reached the goal. He's the Victor, and because we're in Him, we're victors too!

Psalm 119:162 says, "I rejoice at Your word as one who finds great treasure." That means we can act like the Bible is true even when we don't feel like it...even when it doesn't look like it...even when everything around us seems to be saying, "This isn't working for me!"

One person who was famous for declaring victory in advance was football Hall of Fame Quarterback Joe Namath. When his team went to the 1969 Super Bowl he announced before the game even started that they were going to win. I once saw him interviewed on television about it and he said, at the time, His coach and some of his fellow players objected to his announcement. "What are you doing?" they said. "Now the opposing team is really going have it in for you." But Joe didn't pay any attention to their complaints. He stuck by his statement and, sure enough, his team won.

As a believer, you can take much the same approach to the things of the spirit. You can prime your inner pump by declaring your victory and acknowledging "every good thing which is in you in Christ Jesus."[35] You can stir up your faith by shouting over the fact that everything Jesus purchased through His death and resurrection 2,000 years ago is already yours.

After you've shouted though, after you've meditated and confessed the Word and spent time praying in other tongues, you'll want to get quiet. You'll want to listen to

---

35 Philemon 1:6 KJV

your spirit.

## An Inward Knowing

"But exactly what should I listen for?" you might ask. "Should I expect to hear a voice?"

Not necessarily. God's primary way of communicating with us as His children is through what the Bible refers to as the "witness" of the Spirit.

> For as many as are led by the Spirit of God, these are sons of God. For you did not receive the spirit of bondage again to fear, but you received the Spirit of adoption by whom we cry out, "Abba, Father." The Spirit Himself bears witness with our spirit that we are children of God, (Rom. 8:14-15)

Notice those verses say the Holy Spirit *bears witness* with our spirit. In other words, He gives us a knowing on the inside that something is right or true. As a believer, you're familiar with this kind of knowing because, as those verses point out, you've already experienced it in connection with your salvation.

Think about it for a moment. How do you know you're saved? Is it because you mentally remember a time when you prayed the sinner's prayer or because you wrote down the date in your Bible?

No, if you've truly received Jesus as your Lord and Savior, you know you're saved because you can sense it down on the inside of you. Your spirit bears witness with the Holy Spirit and says, "God is my very own Father and

I am His child!" You may not be able to explain to other people exactly how you know this is true, but you know it nevertheless.

If you don't have this witness within you, I encourage you to stop right now and act on Romans 10:9. It says, "That if thou shalt confess with thy mouth the Lord Jesus, and shalt believe in thine heart that God hath raised him from the dead, thou shalt be saved. For with the heart man believeth unto righteousness; and with the mouth confession is made unto salvation."

The instant you put your faith in Jesus and declare His Lordship over your life, you'll be born again. You'll become part of the family of God, and when Jesus comes to take His family to heaven you'll get to go. That's important because the Bible says:

> As in the days before the flood, they were eating and drinking, marrying and giving in marriage, until the day that Noah entered the ark, and did not know until the flood came and took them all away, so also will the coming of the Son of Man be. Then two men will be in the field: one will be taken and the other left. Two women will be grinding at the mill: one will be taken and the other left. Watch therefore, for you do not know what hour your Lord is coming. (Matt. 24:42)

You don't want to be one of those who are left behind when Jesus returns and Christians start disappearing from offices, shopping malls, and airplanes. You don't want to be saying to yourself, "Now what was that prayer in Romans that I intended to pray? I never got around to it." No, you want to be saying, "I'm out of here!"

In other words, you want to be ready.

Think about a husband whose wife is pregnant and about to have her child. He's not going to wait until her water breaks to start preparing to go to the hospital. He won't wait until the contractions are 30 seconds apart to start packing the overnight bag, hunting for the car keys, and stop by the gas station. That's too late. He's going to be prepared so he can get out of there fast!

That's how you want to be when Jesus comes. You want to be prepared. You want to have the witness within you that you've already "passed from death unto life"[36] and you're a child of God.

"Well, I'm saved all right," you might say, "I have the witness of it in my spirit and I know that when the time comes I'll go to heaven. I'm just not sure if I can be led by the Spirit in the meantime as I go about my daily life."

Certainly you can! Jesus said so. In the tenth chapter of John, He described Himself as the Good Shepherd and identified those of us who believe in Him as His sheep. The Shepherd leads the sheep, He said, "and the sheep follow him, for they know his voice. They will by no means follow a stranger, but will flee from him, for they do not know the voice of strangers...My sheep hear My voice, and I know them, and they follow Me."[37]

---

36  1 John 3:14
37  John 10:4-5, 27

## TAPPING INTO WISDOM'S TREASURES

According to Jesus, you are perfectly able to hear and identify His voice. He has given you that ability so that you can follow Him. As long as you're listening to Him for that purpose, you'll be able pick up on His leadings. And the more you pick up on them, the more familiar to you His voice will become.

As you continue to follow Him, you'll begin to discern more easily where He wants you to go and what He wants you to do. You'll spend less time spinning your mental wheels trying to figure things out on your own and more time following the instructions in Proverbs 3:

> Trust in the LORD with all your heart, and lean not on your own understanding; in all your ways acknowledge Him, and He shall direct your paths. (vv. 5-6)

### Keeping God's Wisdom on Tap

One person in my life who showed me what it looks like to trust the Lord and lean not to my own understanding was my mother. She always kept her spiritual pump primed so no matter what surprises life handed her, she always had God's wisdom on tap. As a result, she didn't always respond to disturbing situations in what you might call a "typical" manner.

Take, for example, the sad night my niece was killed in a car accident. She'd been driving late at night and fallen asleep at the wheel. She wasn't wearing her seatbelt so she was thrown out of the car and pinned underneath it. She was only 32 years old and her death was not the will of the

Lord. But the devil took advantage of the circumstances and used them to steal, kill, and destroy.

My sister had called me in the middle of the night to tell me what had happened, and after ministering to her, the next morning I went to my mother's house to break the news. When I told her that her granddaughter had died, she paused for a moment and just sat there in silence. Then she said the unexpected.

"Hallelujah!"

Certainly, she wasn't praising God that her granddaughter had been killed in a car accident. She was rejoicing because she saw life from a different perspective. She knew that when a Christian dies, they're in heaven, that to be absent from the body is to be present with the Lord.[38] She was confident that heaven is real, her granddaughter was there, and God's grace was sufficient for our family in this situation.

My mother didn't have to go fast and seek the Lord for a week to locate His wisdom. She was always prayed up. So she yielded to the witness of the Holy Spirit within her and out of her innermost being came praise to God.

I remember another such time when my mother was in her late eighties. She was living in a guest house on our property and she walked out to the road where the mailbox was to get the mail. She'd made the trek many times without a problem. But on that particular day she tripped over a little piece of wrought iron by the gate and fell face first

---

38  2 Corinthians 5:8: "We are confident, yes, well pleased rather to be absent from the body and to be present with the Lord."

onto the concrete.

    I was in the house when the doorbell rang. Wondering who it was, I opened the door and there she stood with a big knot on her head. Her face was already beginning to swell. I knew it wasn't good at any age to knock your head against the concrete, and at eighty years old it was particularly dangerous. So I gently, but quickly, guided her in the house, sat her down, and started praying.

    As soon as I started to pray, the Holy Spirit jumped right up on the inside of her. She started praising the Lord and confessing His healing Word. I took her to the doctor; he checked her out and said she was just fine. All was well.

    That's what can happen when you stay spiritually primed. You can instantly trust in the Lord. You don't have to lean to your own understanding and say, "This doesn't look good. There's going to be a problem here." You don't have to wait three days while the situation grows worse, then go to the doctor, get a bad report, and go through all kinds of turbulent emotions.

    No, if you'll stay filled with the Holy Spirit and full of God's Word, you can get quiet and listen to your spirit anytime, anyplace, in any circumstances. You can draw on God's wisdom whenever you need it because you always have it on tap.

## More Valuable Than Gold

    Of course, to draw on God's wisdom you can't be a know-it-all. You have to be willing to acknowledge your dependence on the Lord and seek His help and direction. You must have some humility. That's why Proverbs 3 says:

> Do not be wise in your own eyes; fear the LORD and depart from evil. It will be health to your flesh, and strength to your bones. (v. 7-8)

Humility is a small price to pay for the riches of God's wisdom. His wisdom is the most valuable thing you could ever possess. It's kind of like the gold they advertise on television these days. Have you seen those commercials? They go on and on about how valuable gold is and about how it can protect you in times of economic disaster. The announcer warns in scary tones about the uncertainty of your financial future and says, "If you don't buy gold now, you may lose everything!"

Such marketing techniques may be dramatic but much of what those ads say about gold is actually true—and according to the Bible, God's wisdom is even better than gold. It will not only enable us to increase financially and secure our economic future, it will bring us blessing in every other area of life as well. Proverbs 3:13-18 confirms this. It says:

> Happy is the man who finds wisdom, and the man who gains understanding; for her proceeds are better than the profits of silver, and her gain than fine gold. She is more precious than rubies, and all the things you may desire cannot compare with her. Length of days is in her right hand, in her left hand riches and honor. Her ways are ways of pleasantness, and

all her paths are peace. She is a tree of life to those who take hold of her, and happy are all who retain her. (Prov. 3:13-18)

The world's wisdom can't do what God's wisdom can. It might bring you riches but not honor. It might help you make a lot of money but rob you of your family, your friends, and your health.

With God's wisdom, however, you can have it all! You can gain wealth with integrity. You can do business in an honorable way that blesses people and draws them to you. Instead of stressing out over your money and dying young, you can live a long, pleasant, peaceful life.

So take some time to tap into the treasure that's inside you. Invest some moments and some hours getting quiet and listening to your spirit. I guarantee, it's the best investment you'll ever make.

## *Confession*

My spirit is the candle of the Lord. He illuminates it with His wisdom. Because I am a child of God, my spirit within me bears witness with the Holy Spirit to God's truth. I hear the voice of the Good Shepherd in my heart. He leads me and I follow Him. I don't lean on my own understanding. I trust Him in all my ways and keep my spirit primed so I always have His wisdom on tap!

## *Summary Questions*

1. What did you learn from Elijah's experience with the wind, the earthquake, and the fire?

2. Why does the Bible refer to the spirit of man as "the candle of the Lord"?

3. What is the primary way the Holy Spirit leads God's children?

4. How can you be certain you'll hear the voice of the Lord?

5. What should you do when you have trouble accessing the deep waters of your spirit? How can you prime your spiritual pump?

# Chapter 6
## The Secret of Supernatural Success

*Therefore whoever hears these sayings of Mine, and does them, I will liken him to a wise man who built his house on the rock.*
Matthew 7:24

Thus far we've talked about four ways of tapping into the wealth of divine knowledge and understanding that belongs to us in Christ. They include praying for it, meditating and confessing the Word, praying in other tongues, and listening to our spirit. But before we conclude this study I want to add one more element. It's a fifth way to access the wisdom of God, and it's so important that everything else we've discussed in this book depends on it.

What is this vital element?

It's obedience.

## TAPPING INTO WISDOM'S TREASURES

When it comes to enjoying the benefits of God's wisdom, obedience is absolutely essential. It's what produces practical results in our lives. Although receiving God's wisdom is wonderful, acting on it—doing what God tells us to do and following the leadings He gives us through His quiet, inner witness in our spirit—is truly the ultimate secret to supernatural success. Joshua 1:8 makes this very clear. It says:

> This Book of the Law shall not depart from your mouth, but you shall meditate in it day and night, that you may observe to do according to all that is written in it. For then you will make your way prosperous, and then you will have good success.

When we looked at this scripture previously, we focused on what it says about meditating, or muttering and speaking the Word. But here I want to emphasize again the purpose of such meditation: We're to engage in it not only so we can *observe* (or see) what God is showing us, but so we can *do* it, because the doing is what brings us *good success*!

The word *success* in Hebrew means *to deal wisely or follow the wisdom of God, to walk the path that He has prepared for us*. It refers to taking action. It speaks of not just knowing but living our lives in accordance with every aspect of God's Word.

His Word does have different aspects, you know. As the Apostle Paul said, it has been given to us "by inspiration of God, and is profitable for doctrine, for reproof, for correction, for instruction in righteousness."[39] Most all of us enjoy being edified and enlightened by God's Word. We like to receive revelation from it. But we aren't always as excited when the Word reproves us. Sometimes we'd rather skip that part.

To stay on the path God has prepared for us, however, we must embrace all of His Word. If we take the inspiration side and ignore the correction side we'll get into trouble. Our lives will veer off course. Then we'll need even more reproof! Every time we open the Bible it will seem like the Holy Spirit is using it to correct us.

To understand this, think of the navigation system in a car. It's designed to get you where you need to go. As long as you're on track, you might travel for miles without receiving much input from the system. If you miss a turn, however, the vocal activity on your GPS will increase. It will start telling you what to do to rectify your mistake. It will keep talking to you and re-directing you until you get back on the right route.

God does the same thing for us. He keeps us on the right path by giving us directions through His written Word and by the Holy Spirit. If we start to stray, He starts talking to us a little more. He keeps trying to realign and redirect us because the slightest detour can put us on a destructive path. And the farther we go down that path, the less clearly we'll hear the voice of God. Eventually, we can end up going full speed ahead, thinking we're going the right way when actually we're not!

---

39  2 Timothy 3:16-17

# TAPPING INTO WISDOM'S TREASURES

In other words, we can become deceived.

## Be Sure to Look in the Mirror

Deception is dangerous. If we allow ourselves to fall prey to it, it can completely thwart God's plan for our lives. That's why we should pay special attention to the instructions in James 1:21-24:

> Lay aside all filthiness and overflow of wickedness, and receive with meekness the implanted word, which is able to save your souls. But be doers of the word, and not hearers only, deceiving yourselves. For if anyone is a hearer of the word and not a doer, he is like a man observing his natural face in a mirror; for he observes himself, goes away, and immediately forgets what kind of man he was. But he who looks into the perfect law of liberty and continues in it, and is not a forgetful hearer but a doer of the work, this one will be blessed in what he does.

Notice the first thing this passage tells us to do to avoid deception is to lay aside (or rid ourselves of) "all filthiness and overflow of wickedness." That would include anything that's sinful or displeasing to the Lord. It would include not only ungodly activities and attitudes but also unnecessary weights and distractions that can slow us down in our Christian race and hinder our spiritual effectiveness.[40]

---

40 Hebrews 12:1:"Therefore then, since we are surrounded by so great a cloud of witnesses [who have borne testimony to the Truth] let us strip off and throw

How can you discern what those things are? How can you differentiate between what's hindering you and what's helpful in promoting God's will in your life?

According to this passage, you do it by "receiving with meekness the implanted word, which is able to save your souls."

As you already know, your soul consists of your mind, your will, and your emotions. It's the natural or psychological part of your being. (The Greek word for *soul* is *pseuche*, which is where we get our English word *psyche*.) According to 1 Corinthians 2:14, your soul doesn't have the capacity to receive revelations from God. His truth must be "spiritually discerned," which means it must be received by your spirit.

This doesn't mean, however, that God's Word doesn't have any impact on your soul. On the contrary, your soul is profoundly affected by it. When your spirit is enlightened by the Truth, understanding comes to your mind. Your thinking and your perspective on life is changed. It becomes easier for you to make right decisions and godly choices. Because you understand God's will and His ways you can think like He does and see things from His point of view.

But, as this passage says, that's not all there is to living a blessed life. You have to do more than just hear the Word, quote Bible verses, and say, "I understand that." You

---

aside every encumbrance (unnecessary weight) and that sin which so readily (deftly and cleverly) cling to and entangles us, and let us run with patient endurance and steady active persistence the appointed course that is set before us." (AMP)

have to tie your knowledge to action. Otherwise you'll be like a person who looks at himself in the mirror and then walks away and forgets what he looks like.

You don't want to be that kind of person!

You proved it when you were getting dressed this morning. Most likely you looked at yourself in the mirror several times. First, you looked at the front side of yourself. Then you may have turned around and looked at the back side. You might have even checked your reflection from all different angles to make sure you were presentable in every way.

Why did you do this? So you could make the necessary adjustments and you wouldn't go through your day looking like a mess.

You'll do the same thing tomorrow because you know it's not enough just to look at yourself in the mirror once and then forget about it. If you want to properly maintain your appearance, you must go back to the mirror again and again.

Spiritually, you want to do the same with the Word of God. You want to keep looking into it because if you don't, you'll forget who you are in Christ. You'll forget you're a new creation; you're the righteousness of God; and you're filled with His life. You'll forget you belong to Jesus and you're not your own; you've been bought with a price. You'll start thinking, *I can just do whatever I want to do*. Then things will start to get ugly and you won't even notice.

I've seen it happen to believers many times over the years. They think they're doing okay spiritually, so they stop looking in the mirror of the Word. They coast along assuming everything is fine and then a challenge arises. A temptation hits or the pressures of life start to squeeze them and they fall apart because spiritually they're a mess.

They haven't been feeding on the Scriptures so their inner man is malnourished. They haven't exercised by acting on God's Word so their spirit is weak. They're in very bad spiritual shape and they haven't even realized it because they've been deceived!

Deception is believing you're on one road when in reality you're on another. It's like driving north on I-15 from Las Vegas and thinking you're going to end up in Los Angeles. It doesn't matter how convinced you are that you're going the right direction, you won't reach your intended destination. It's not going to happen.

You can dream about it. You can think about it. You can call your wife and say, "I'm headed to L.A." But you're not going to get there. Instead you'll have to call your wife at the end of the day and explain to her why you're checking into a hotel in Salt Lake City. You'll have to tell her you ended up there because you were deceived and went the wrong way.

If you don't want that kind of thing to happen to you while you're traveling down the path of life, steer clear of deception. Keep the Word in front of you all the time. Don't just give it a casual glance now and then. Keep it constantly before you.

The Old Testament Israelites did this by wearing little Scripture boxes on their foreheads and on their arms.

## TAPPING INTO WISDOM'S TREASURES

But as New Testament believers we can do something far better. Instead of wearing Scripture boxes on the outside, we can have God's Word dwelling richly on the inside. We can read, listen to, and meditate on the Word until it fills our hearts and overflows into our conduct. Then we'll be totally free from deception and we'll be blessed in what we do!

### Ready for the Storm

Jesus taught about this often during His earthly ministry. In Matthew 7, for instance, He explained it in the form of a parable. He said:

> Whoever hears these sayings of Mine, and does them, I will liken him to a wise man who built his house on the rock: and the rain descended, the floods came, and the winds blew and beat on that house; and it did not fall, for it was founded on the rock. But everyone who hears these sayings of Mine, and does not do them, will be like a foolish man who built his house on the sand: and the rain descended, the floods came, and the winds blew and beat on that house; and it fell. And great was its fall." (vv. 24-27)

I like the fact that Jesus began this parable with the word *whoever*. It tells me that anybody can do this. Anybody can be wise if they'll hear and act on what God says.

That doesn't mean a person can be wise simply by doing something they *think* God said. Many people think they've heard from Him when they really haven't. Then they end up getting in trouble because what thought they heard is actually contrary to the Scriptures.

Always remember, the primary way God is going to guide you is through His written Word. So it should always be your standard. As long as you stick close to the Word, you'll be able to distinguish between the leadings of the Holy Spirit and the pull of your own emotions. You'll be able to divide, as Hebrews 4:12 says, soul and spirit, and see the truth about the thoughts and intents of your heart.

Although I mentioned this in a previous chapter, it bears repeating. There's a very thin line between soul and your spirit, and you need to keep it defined because on occasion, you can be so bombarded by your natural thoughts and feelings, you get confused. You can start wondering, *Is this a leading of the Lord I need to act on? Or is this a temptation of the devil I should resist?*

If you're strong in the written Word of God you'll be able to answer such questions. What the Scriptures say about walking in love will come to your mind, for instance, and the truth will become obvious. You'll think, *That leading isn't from the Lord because it isn't in line with love!*

This is why Jesus compared building your life on God's written Word to building your house on a rock: The Word provides you with a solid foundation!

If you know anything about construction, you understand how important a foundation is. If it's not solid, nothing that's built on it will be right either. The whole structure will be shaky.

## TAPPING INTO WISDOM'S TREASURES

A shaky spiritual structure won't stand up under the pressure of adversity so it inevitably leads to disaster because adversity is an unavoidable fact of life. In this fallen world, storms are always going to come. Floods are going to rage. Winds are going to blow. Regardless of whether you build on the sand or on the Rock, bad things are going to occur.

Certainly, you don't want those kinds of things to happen. You don't pray for them to happen or even expect them to happen. But they happen anyway because what Jesus said is true: "In this world you will have trouble..."

The key to consistently overcoming that trouble is preparing for it in advance by building a solid foundation of the Word of God. Sadly, however, many Christians don't do this. They wait until the rain is falling and then start hunting for their Bible. They wait until the winds are howling to start their spiritual building program.

Think what would have happened if Noah had done that! The flood he faced was the worst one ever. Today we can't even imagine what it was like. About all we have to compare it to here in America is the flood that hit New Orleans some years ago during Hurricane Katrina. Like me, you probably watched it on television. It was devastating. People died. Entire neighborhoods were swept away. Thousands of people had to be evacuated.

If Noah had waited until things like that were happening around him to start building the ark, he and his family would have perished with everybody else. They would have had no hope of escape, but Noah was prepared.

He'd already heard and obeyed the Word of God. He'd built his life—and the ark—on the Rock long before the first clap of thunder was heard. He'd started his construction project when the sun was shining and there wasn't a cloud in the sky.

As a wise believer, you'll follow his example. You won't wait until calamity strikes to hear and obey God's Word. You'll make it the foundation of your life right now by meditating daily on what the Lord is saying to you through the Scriptures. You'll start in advance assimilating His Word into your experience and turning it into action in your everyday life. Then, when adversities arise, you can stand tall.

I'm thinking right now of the beach houses I used to see on the coast of North Carolina where I grew up. They were constructed on top of stilts so that when storms swept in from the ocean they wouldn't be damaged by the high waters. But the stilts didn't just rest on the sand. Because sand tends to shift and wash away, the builders would drill down until they found ground solid enough to provide a strong foundation. Then they'd set the stilts in that foundation so the houses would not only tower above the biggest waves, they'd be strong enough to withstand hurricane force winds.

Believers who build their lives on Jesus Christ and the Word of God are much like those houses. Their foundation is so deep and solid that the winds of this world can't blow them down. When the storms of adversity hit, the Rock holds them stable. It keeps them secure. Yet because they're also seated with Christ in heavenly places, the tides of adversity can't overwhelm them. They tower in victory over even the highest tides.

Believers who neglect to build on the Word, however, don't fare as well. When crises hit and times get turbulent, their foundation crumbles. And like the sandy-ground house in Jesus' parable, great is their fall.

**A Lesson Learned the Hard Way**

One Old Testament character who saw his life crumble and experienced a great fall was Saul, the first king of Israel. He learned firsthand how costly it can be to disregard and disobey the Word of the Lord.

The setting for his lesson was his battle with the Amalekites. Before it began, God gave him explicit instructions. He commanded Saul to completely wipe out all the Amalekites and to destroy all their livestock. (God told him to do this because if he didn't, it would cause a problem for Israel in the future.)

As king, Saul was responsible to obey God's commands, but after the battle was won, he came up with his own plan. Instead of killing all Amalekites, he decided to spare the life of their king as well as some of their animals.

The prophet Samuel was the priest of Israel at the time so God spoke to him about Saul's disobedient actions. He said:

"I greatly regret that I have set up Saul as king,
for he has turned back from following Me,

and has not performed My commandments." And it grieved Samuel, and he cried out to the LORD all night...Then Samuel went to Saul and...said, "When you were little in your own eyes, were you not head of the tribes of Israel? And did not the LORD anoint you king over Israel?...Why then did you not obey the voice of the LORD? Why did you swoop down on the spoil, and do evil in the sight of the LORD?" (1 Sam. 15:11, 17, 19)

Notice what opened the door for Saul's disobedience was the fact that he stopped being "little in his own sight." In other words, he lost his humility. That's a pitfall every Christian must beware of because any of us at any stage of our spiritual development can stumble into it.

I remember hearing Oral Roberts say that when God began to use him in the ministry of miracles and healings his mother told him, "Son, be sure to stay little in your own eyes." Brother Roberts said he never forgot those words. And if you want to establish your life on the Rock of God's wisdom, you won't forget them either. Regardless of how long you walk with the Lord, you'll keep on receiving "with meekness" (or with humility) His "implanted word."[41]

You won't approach the Scriptures as if you already know everything they have to say. You'll approach them with a hungry and humble heart. You'll say, "Lord, I want to learn and grow. I want to see your Word like I've never seen it before. I want to know Jesus better and have a deeper

---
41  James 1:21, KJV

understanding of Your ways."

Most believers start out with this attitude when they first get saved. Because they're aware of how little they know spiritually and how dependent they are on the Lord, they read their Bible and go to church at every opportunity. But after a while some believers adopt a more casual approach. They start thinking, *I don't really need to read the Bible and pray every day. I don't need to go to church. Those things aren't necessary for me.*

Believers who entertain such thoughts are no longer little in their own eyes. They think they know more about what's good for them than God does, but they're seriously mistaken. If God says we need to meditate on the Word day and night, then we do! If He says we need to pray, we do! If He says it's necessary for us to be connected to the local church, and we need ministry gifts such as pastors and teachers to help us grow strong in the Word of God and develop spiritually, we do!

God always knows best.

Saul found this out the hard way. He decided he knew better than God did how to deal with the Amalekites' king and livestock. When Samuel confronted him about it, instead of admitting he was wrong Saul did what all of us have done at one time or another. He tried to talk his way out of trouble. He said:

> But I have obeyed the voice of the LORD, and gone on the mission on which the LORD sent me, and brought back Agag king of Amalek; I have utterly destroyed the Amalekites. But

> the people took of the plunder, sheep and oxen, the best of the things which should have been utterly destroyed, to sacrifice to the LORD your God in Gilgal. (vv. 20-21)

This is how Saul defended his actions. He basically said to Samuel, "I did *part* of what the Lord said." Then he blamed the Israelites. And finally, he justified himself by talking about the sacrifices he'd made to the Lord.

Samuel, however, didn't buy Saul's excuses. He said:

> Has the LORD as great delight in burnt offerings and sacrifices, as in obeying the voice of the LORD? Behold, to obey is better than sacrifice, And to heed than the fat of rams. For rebellion is as the sin of witchcraft, and stubbornness is as iniquity and idolatry. (vv. 22-23)

This is as true in our lives as believers today as it was in Saul's: Partial obedience is *not* obedience. And no amount of sacrifice can compensate for ignoring God's Word. Obeying Him wholeheartedly is better than anything else we can do!

If we don't have specific, individualized instructions from the Lord about how He wants us to serve Him, we can just obey the general guidance of the Scriptures. We can simply put our hand to something that seems good. We don't have to hear a voice from heaven to be an usher at church or to work in the nursery. We can just choose on our own to do those things as an offering unto the Lord.

## TAPPING INTO WISDOM'S TREASURES

But when He gives us a specific command, we want to follow it exactly. We don't want to improvise and come up with something else we think is better. We want to do precisely what He said because if we deviate even a little bit from the path He has charted for us, the farther we go, the more off course we'll be.

We can see evidence of this in the story of Saul. He got so far off the road of blessing that Samuel had to say to him:

> Because you have rejected the word of the LORD, He also has rejected you from being king." (v. 23)

I don't want that to happen to me, do you? I don't want to travel half my life on the right road and then get off course. I don't want to serve Him for twenty years, then lose my anointing and miss out on my divine destiny because of disobedience. So I've made up my mind: I'm going to stay on course by obeying God's Word and choosing to walk in His wisdom every day.

"But Pastor David," you might say, "what if I've already gotten off track? What if I've spent years building my life on the sand instead of on the Rock?"

Make a change! Tap into God's wisdom right now and get back on the path He has prepared for you. Start rebuilding your life by laying a new foundation. Become not just a hearer of the Word but a doer.

Then you won't be washed away by the floods of this world. When the winds of adversity blow and the water rises, you'll have the Word of God to steady you. Having done all to stand, you'll be able to stand.

> ...having girded your waist with truth, having put on the breastplate of righteousness, and having shod your feet with the preparation of the gospel of peace; above all, taking the shield of faith with which you will be able to quench all the fiery darts of the wicked one. (Eph. 6:14-16)

Instead of being deceived into going the wrong direction, you'll be in the right place at the right time doing the right thing with the right people. You'll be blessed coming in and blessed going out...all because you walked in the wisdom of God.

## TAPPING INTO WISDOM'S TREASURES

### *Confession*

I am a doer of God's Word and not a hearer only so I am blessed in what I do. I stand strong and victorious through every storm because His Word is my strong foundation. When the storms of adversity hit, Jesus, my Rock, makes me stable. I obey Him and He keeps me secure. Seated with Him in heavenly places, I overcome every trouble and rise above every flood. I continue in His Word and His truth makes me free.

### *Summary Questions*

1. What is the fifth way of tapping into the wisdom of God? Why is it so important?

2. What is deception and what can you do to avoid it?

3. How can you distinguish between the leadings of the Holy Spirit and the pull of your soul?

4. Why does a shaky spiritual foundation inevitably lead to disaster?

5. What attitude opened the door to Saul's disobedience? How do believers sometimes fall prey to it today?

# Scriptures

## Joshua 1:8

This book of the law shall not depart out of thy mouth; but thou shalt meditate therein day and night, that thou mayest observe to do according to all that is written therein: for then thou shalt make thy way prosperous, and then thou shalt have good success.

## Job 32:8

But *there is* a spirit in man, And the breath of the Almighty gives him understanding.

## Proverbs 3:5-8

Trust in the LORD with all your heart, And lean not on your own understanding;
[6] In all your ways acknowledge Him, And He shall direct your paths.
[7] Do not be wise in your own eyes; Fear the LORD and depart from evil.
[8] It will be health to your flesh, And strength to your bones

## Proverbs 4:7-9

Wisdom is the principal thing; Therefore get wisdom. And in all your getting, get understanding.
[8] Exalt her, and she will promote you; She will bring you honor, when you embrace her.
[9] She will place on your head an ornament of grace; A crown of glory she will deliver to you."

## TAPPING INTO WISDOM'S TREASURES

**Proverbs 20:5**

Counsel in the heart of man *is like* deep water, But a man of understanding will draw it out.

**Proverbs 20:27**

The spirit of a man is the lamp of the Lord, Searching all the inner depths of his heart.

**Proverbs 3:13-18**

Happy is the man who finds wisdom, And the man who gains understanding;
[14] For her proceeds are better than the profits of silver, And her gain than fine gold.
[15] She is more precious than rubies, And all the things you may desire cannot compare with her.
[16] Length of days is in her right hand, In her left hand riches and honor.
[17] Her ways are ways of pleasantness, And all her paths are peace.
[18] She is a tree of life to those who take hold of her, And happy are all who retain her.

**Matthew 7:24**

Therefore whosoever heareth these sayings of mine, and doeth them, I will liken him unto a wise man, which built his house upon a rock:

**John 10:4-5, 27**

And when he putteth forth his own sheep, he goeth before

them, and the sheep follow him: for they know his voice.
⁵ And a stranger will they not follow, but will flee from him: for they know not the voice of strangers.
²⁷ My sheep hear my voice, and I know them, and they follow me:

### John 14:26
But the Helper, the Holy Spirit, whom the Father will send in My name, He will teach you all things, and bring to your remembrance all things that I said to you.

### Romans 8:14-15
For as many as are led by the Spirit of God, these are sons of God.
¹⁵ For you did not receive the spirit of bondage again to fear, but you received the Spirit of adoption by whom we cry out, "Abba, Father."

### Romans 8:26-27
Likewise the Spirit also helps in our weaknesses. For we do not know what we should pray for as we ought, but the Spirit Himself makes intercession for us with groanings which cannot be uttered.
²⁷ Now He who searches the hearts knows what the mind of the Spirit is, because He makes intercession for the saints according to the will of God.

### 1 Corinthians 1:30
But of Him you are in Christ Jesus, who became for us

wisdom from God—and righteousness and sanctification and redemption.

## 1 Corinthians 2:11-12, 14

For what man knows the things of a man except the spirit of the man which is in him? Even so no one knows the things of God except the Spirit of God.
[12] Now we have received, not the spirit of the world, but the Spirit who is from God, that we might know the things that have been freely given to us by God.
[14] But the natural man does not receive the things of the Spirit of God, for they are foolishness to him; nor can he know them, because they are spiritually discerned

## Ephesians 1:7-8

In Him we have redemption through His blood, the forgiveness of sins, according to the riches of His grace [8] which He made to abound toward us in all wisdom and prudence.

## James 3:17

But the wisdom that is from above is first pure, then peaceable, gentle, willing to yield, full of mercy and good fruits, without partiality and without hypocrisy.

## 1 John 2:20, 26-27

But you have an anointing from the Holy One, and you know all things.
[26] These things I have written to you concerning those who

try to deceive you.

²⁷ But the anointing which you have received from Him abides in you, and you do not need that anyone teach you; but as the same anointing teaches you concerning all things, and is true, and is not a lie, and just as it has taught you, you will abide in Him.

# How To Be Born Again

The way to get *in Christ* is to be born again. Jesus said that it is a person's spirit that must be born again. This miracle, by the Holy Spirit, will happen within you the moment you call on Jesus to be your personal Lord and Savior. God is now offering you a new life, and an eternal home in Heaven with Him. It's as simple as A, B, C:

**Acknowledge that you are a sinner, separated from God, and in need of salvation.**
For all have sinned and fall short of the glory of God. (Romans 3:23)

**Believe that Jesus Christ, the Son of God, died for your sins and rose again from the dead.**
But God demonstrates His own love toward us, in that while we were still sinners, Christ died for us. (Romans 5:8)

**Confess (say) with your mouth, "Jesus is Lord!"**
That if you confess with your mouth the Lord Jesus and believe in your heart that God has raised him from the dead, you will be saved. (Romans 10:9)

To receive Jesus as your Lord and Savior simply pray this prayer:

> **God in heaven, I turn from sin to You. I believe in my heart that Jesus died for my sin and rose again. Jesus, come into my life and be my Lord. Thank you for saving me. Today, I am born again! Amen.**

If you prayed the prayer to receive Jesus Christ as your Lord and Savior, please contact us on the web at www.wordoflifelv.com, by email, info@wordoflifelv.com, call us at (702) 645-1990 ext. 101 or write us at: Word of Life Christian Center, 3520 N. Buffalo Dr., Las Vegas, Nevada 89129.

# NOTES

# NOTES

# NOTES

Experience David Shearin's audio or video messages
on Tapping Into Wisdom's Treasures

## Tapping Into Wisdom's Treasures CD and DVD series

Other Books By David Shearin:
The Master Key: Unlock the Mystery of Supernatural Living

To order this or other products by David Shearin visit us on the web @ www.thewordforliving.com or call (866) 700-9673

### Television Broadcast:
#### The Word For Living
Sundays 7:00 AM Channel 17 UHF/Cable 119
9:00 AM Channel 33 Cable 6
9:30 AM The Church Channel
Check the website for additional listings

### Church Services:
#### Word of Life Christian Center
Sundays @ 8:00am, 10:30am & 6:30pm Wednesdays @ 7:00pm
3520 N. Buffalo Dr. • Las Vegas, NV 89129

Phone: (702) 645-1990 • Fax: (702) 645-3641

E-mail: info@wordoflifelasvegas.com
Visit us on the web @ **www.wordoflifelv.com**
or **www.thewordforliving.com**

### ALSO AVAILABLE BY PASTOR DAVID SHEARIN...

# THE MASTER KEY

## UNLOCK THE MYSTERY OF SUPERNATURAL LIVING

Available in Book, Sermons on CD or DVD, Parts 1 & 2. Order online at www.thewordforliving.com

# About The Author

David and Vicki Shearin are the founders and Pastors of Word of Life Christian Center in Las Vegas, Nevada. The church has grown from 5 people to over 2,000 and continues to reach out through various ministries, including a weekly television broadcast, The Word For Living. Possessing the heart of a true shepherd, David is known as a man of integrity and compassion as well as a dynamic preacher and teacher of God's Word. David is the founder of Word of Life Christian Academy, educating children academically and spiritually, Pre-K through High School. He also established Word of Life Bible Institute, which offers a course of study that trains lay people for effective involvement in the ministry of the local church and a degree program that equips men and women for full time ministry.

David and Vicki are graduates of RHEMA Bible Training College and have been in full time ministry for over 32 years. In addition to pastoring, they minister in churches, conferences and Bible Schools throughout the U.S. and in other nations. They have one daughter, Ashley.

www.ingramcontent.com/pod-product-compliance
Lightning Source LLC
Chambersburg PA
CBHW071521080526
44588CB00011B/1514